D A N C E

DANCE FOR EXPORT

Cultural Diplomacy and the Cold War

Naima Prevots

Introduction by Eric Foner

WESLEYAN UNIVERSITY PRESS
Middletown, Connecticut

Wesleyan University Press
Middletown, CT 06459
© 1998 by Naima Prevots
Printed in the United States of America   5 4 3 2
CIP data appear at the end of the book

First Wesleyan paperback 2001

Originally produced in hardcover in 1998 by
Wesleyan/University Press of New England
Hanover, NH 03755

Contents

Acknowledgments

An enormous debt of gratitude goes first and foremost to Lynn Garafola, who encouraged me, always asked tough questions, and proved to be a meticulous, insightful, and supportive colleague and editor. When the various drafts came back with corrections and comments, it was gratifying to know that her high standards and her willingness to put in enormous amounts of time to attain them, would help me produce a better book. I was also fortunate to have Eric Foner read the various drafts; his knowledge and editorial skills played a significant role in clarifying the material into a cogent and meaningful manuscript.

I am grateful to Harriet Mayor Fulbright for her leadership of the Fulbright Association during my first term on the board of directors. It was through my work in that organization that I had the privilege of meeting Senator Fulbright, whose passion for the value of cultural diplomacy has been a guiding light throughout this work. He was responsible for salvaging the classified documents that became the core of this research; when they were destined for the garbage heap, he had them sent to the University of Arkansas, where they now reside. The current executive director, Jane Anderson, was a valued colleague during the three international conferences I chaired, and she encouraged me to form and guide the first Arts Task Force. These activities reinforced my belief in the value of international exchange and understanding.

Most of the research was done in special collections and archives, and the people in charge of these treasure troves proved to be remarkable guides and caring people. My work began in the USIA Historical Collection in Washington, D.C., and Martin Manning was enormously helpful in finding appropriate documents and information. At the University of Arkansas, Michael Dabrishus, as head of Special Collections, made me feel welcome and helped me begin my work with the large collection of material from the State Department and USIA. Betty Austin, the archivist, spent an enormous amount of time answering my questions and charting my course through the numerous boxes that held the information I was seeking to discover and uncover. She not only helped during my stay in Arkansas; she subsequently read drafts of the manuscript and answered numerous phone inquiries.

Jacques Burgering proved to be not only a superb research assistant but also a good friend. He responded with alacrity and intelligence to my emergency requests for more information, and he always managed to find and select the most important material. Lauranell Morris provided superb editorial assistance and was an extremely sensitive and perceptive sounding board. Margaret Bucky was, as always, a caring friend as well as a careful reader; her comments made a big difference as the manuscript developed. Many thanks go to Karla Coghill for her time and patience in retyping and formatting and to Vladimir Anguelov for his enormous help in locating photographs.

I was fortunate to receive a great deal of help from the Eisenhower Library and from the Dance Collection, The New York Public Library for the Performing Arts. Questions and requests were answered immediately, and help was always given with a smile. When I gathered pictures at the Dance Collection, Monica Moseley and Charles Perrier were extremely responsive to my needs. The librarians at American University were wonderful, and I feel privileged to have them as colleagues; no matter what the request, they always came up with the right book or resource. For four years Dave Penoyer was my student research assistant, and he was an invaluable helper. Barbara Palfy, who read an early draft, was most helpful, and I am grateful to Shelley Berg for her thoughtful reading of a later one. I am also grateful to Larry Warren, George Jackson, and Christopher Paddack for agreeing to read the manuscript and giving me valuable feedback. Sally Banes, as president of the Society of Dance History Scholars, played a significant role in helping this manuscript see the light of day.

My children and my husband are an important part of what keeps me going. Many thanks to them for everything.

DANCE FOR EXPORT

Introduction

The Cold War, which so powerfully shaped the lives of two generations of Americans, has faded into history. But it remains a continuing source of fascination for scholars of the recent past. Naima Prevots's study of how dance was caught up in the era's diplomacy is a welcome addition to a burgeoning literature that views the Cold War as a cultural conflict as well as a clash of armies and ideologies. In what Cold Warriors called the "battle for the hearts and minds of men," dance played a small, but fascinating role.

In retrospect, conflict between the Soviet Union and the United States, the two major powers to emerge from World War II, seems to have been almost inevitable. Early in 1946, in his famous Long Telegram from Moscow, American diplomat George Kennan advised the Truman administration that no modus vivendi with the Soviet Union was possible. Two weeks later, in a speech at Fulton, Missouri, Britain's wartime prime minister, Winston Churchill, declared that an "iron curtain" had descended across Europe, partitioning the free West from the communist East. Official embrace of the Cold War as the foundation of American foreign policy came in March 1947, when President Harry S. Truman called for American assistance to "freedom-loving" peoples in a global crusade against communism. The Berlin blockade soon followed, along with, the establishment of NATO (the North Atlantic Treaty Organization), the Korean War, and a long period of hostility between the Soviet bloc and what came to be known as the Free World.

At home, the Cold War produced an anticommunist crusade, an effort to purge American life of both communists and what attorney general Tom C. Clark called "foreign ideologies." The Cold War spawned a spate of public and private efforts against "subversive" elements. Many groups seized upon anticommunism to settle accounts with long-established enemies. Business used it to tar government intervention in the economy with the brush of socialism, physicians to denounce proposals for national health insurance as "socialized medicine." Anticommunism became a tool wielded by Republicans against the legacy of New Deal liberalism, employers against labor unions, white supremacists against black civil rights, and upholders of sexual morality and traditional gender roles against homosexuality and feminism. The world of the arts could not remain immune from these pressures, as old friendships shattered, former comrades testified against one another before congressional committees, and artists enlisted, knowingly or unwittingly, in the battle against the Soviets via such organizations as the Congress for Cultural Freedom.

Like any conflict between great powers, the Cold War was a struggle for public opinion as well as military advantage. The "selling of America" had been a crucial feature of World War I, which produced the Committee on Public Information, and of World War II, in which government agencies and private advertisers energetically promoted President Franklin D. Roosevelt's Four Freedoms. Similarly, the Cold War was not merely a series of military alliances and violent confrontations, but a concerted campaign to promote the "American way of life" throughout the world. Central to this effort was the celebration of "freedom," ostensibly the quality that most fully distinguished American society from the Soviet foe. Indeed, during the Cold War, the idea of the Free World (an expansive ideological construct that embraced democratic nations such as the United States and Great Britain and such unlikely members as fascist Spain and apartheid-divided South Africa) assumed a central place in political discourse.

Cold War freedom had many meanings, from political democracy to the right to worship as one chose. But as recent literature has shown, freedom became increasingly identified with consumer capitalism or, as it was then unfailingly called, "free enterprise." The two decades following the end of World War II witnessed economic expansion and rising living standards on an unprecedented scale. The gross national product more than doubled, and in every measurable way—diet, housing, wages, education, recreation—most Americans lived better than their parents and grandparents had. The celebration of consumer society assumed a prominent place in the cultural Cold War. Recent books have highlighted the numerous industrial expositions showcasing American technology and material prosperity sent overseas by the U.S. government. Beginning with the Chicago Fair of 1950, which included a daily historical pageant entitled "Frontiers of Freedom" and a spectacular if to some eyes rather frightening "march of machines," freedom and consumerism were inextricably linked in these shows. Consumer products provided the best propaganda for the United States, insisted Joseph Barry, a reporter for *House Beautiful* magazine, who waxed rhapsodic over "the freedom offered by washing machines and dishwashers, vacuum cleaners, automobiles, and refrigerators." Indeed, it was at one of the era's expositions of American consumer products that a classic Cold War confrontation over the relative merits of capitalism and communism took place. This was the famous "kitchen debate" between Vice President Richard Nixon and Soviet Premier Nikita S. Khrushchev, at the 1959 American National Exhibition in Moscow, a showcase for American hi-fi sets, home appliances, and automobiles that Russians by the thousands poured in to see.[1]

The "kitchen debate," in which Nixon equated American freedom with material abundance, has become a well-known icon of the Cold War, a tale repeated in virtually every textbook and scholarly work on the period. Less attention has been devoted to the numerous artists sent abroad as "goodwill ambassadors" in an effort to promote a rather more elevated image of American culture. Indeed, some Americans feared that presentations like Nixon's, which glorified the relentless pursuit of material goods, inadvertently reinforced Soviet portrayals of the United States as a society of "gum-chewing, insensitive, materialistic barbarians" (the colorful words of a New Jersey congressman who favored federal sponsorship of the arts).[2]

On the eve of American entry into World War II, in his influential treatise *The American Century*, publisher Henry Luce had predicted a future in which the nation would assume its place as the "dominant power in the world," and an "abundant life" would follow for all mankind. But Luce also observed that "our jazz, movies, slang"—in other words, American popular culture—were as much a source of international power as the country's military might and economic productivity. This proved an extremely prescient insight, although "high" art—especially painting, music, and dance—would shortly assume a place alongside movies, musicals, and top ten songs as weapons in the Cold War.[3]

Cultural diplomacy played a significant and complex role in this overall confrontation. Overseas, the State Department promoted a vision of American culture not universally accepted at home. Even as domestic conservatives condemned abstract expressionism as a subversive plot to undermine homegrown artistic traditions, part and parcel of a "sinister conspiracy conceived in the black heart of Russia" according to one superpatriot in Congress, works by Jackson Pollack and other modern painters were sent overseas. A counterpoint to the socialist realism imposed on Soviet artists, modern art reinforced an image of the United States as the new leader of the avant-garde, and was said to embody the American spirit of enterprise and individual freedom. In dance, even as upholders of public morality criticized choreographers like Martha Graham for works that revolved around the theme of sexuality, the government promoted her company as a reflection of the vitality of American culture and the freedom of individual artists in the United States.[4]

Although recent historians have begun to probe the use of art as a weapon in the Cold War, the intersection of dance and diplomacy has thus far eluded scholarly investigation. Few if any scholars of the Cold War mention the dance touring program, and few historians of dance have placed this episode in the broad context of cultural politics. Here is where Prevots makes a significant contribution. Drawing on a rich array of previously unexamined manuscript material, including State Department records, congressional committee hearings, and the minutes of the dance panel that chose artists to tour overseas, she is able to piece together the inner workings of the dance program and to illuminate the complex set of interests—political, fiscal, artistic—that shaped its evolution. She traces the dance program's development from the establishment in 1954 of President Eisenhower's Emergency Fund for Art through the 1960s.

While the Works Projects Administration had operated a small Dance Project in the 1930s, touring was not part of its mandate. Modern government sponsorship of dance was largely a byproduct of the Cold War and the government's desire to present American culture in a positive light overseas. But among Prevots's more surprising findings is how little politics in the formal Cold War sense affected the choice of which troupes to send abroad. The politics of dance abounded—differences between the "old" and "new" American ballet, between mainstream modern dance and an emerging avant-garde—but the minutes of the Dance Panel suggest that the domestic politics of anticommunism had little impact. In 1947, the Truman administration had established a loyalty review system in which government employees were forced to demonstrate their patriotism. Soon, Congressional committees and counterparts on the state level were calling individuals to testify about their past and present political beliefs. Not only membership in the Communist Party but a history of "sympathetic association" with communists became grounds for being dismissed from employment by government, universities, and many private companies. These were the years of the Hollywood blacklist, and when performers like Paul Robeson and Pete Seeger were deprived of their livelihoods because of their political beliefs. Yet the Dance Panel, dominated by critics and dance professionals based in New York City, where the blacklist was not as severe as elsewhere, unhesitatingly sent overseas dancers—Martha Graham herself being a striking example— whose previous association with left-wing causes would certainly have disqualified them from participation in other government programs.

This is not to say that the dance program was apolitical. Never far from the panelists' minds was the desire to counteract the positive impression created by Soviet touring attractions like the Bolshoi and Moiseyev dance companies. This consideration led to long debates—related by Prevots in lively, ironic prose—about the relative merits of classical ballet and homegrown modern dance as representations of American culture. Should the United States emphasize its indigenous dance achievements— modern dance, traditional folk dance, Native American dance—or its ability to compete with the Soviets on the terrain of classical ballet? Not surprisingly, the first company sent to the Soviet Union was not a modern dance group but the American Ballet Theatre, with a program featuring traditional works like *Les Sylphides*, as well as signature ballets on American themes such as *Rodeo*. The New York City Ballet soon followed, demonstrating that the United States could not only produce dancers as technically accomplished as any in the USSR, but also ballets that surpassed in sophistication and complexity anything seen on a Soviet stage.

Elsewhere, however, the Dance Panel hoped to showcase what it deemed unique in American dance. This was especially true in what had come to be called the Third World. In the eyes of many Asians, Africans, and Latin Americans, violent confrontations over civil rights in the United States—troops in Little Rock, the burning of the buses of freedom riders, the bombing of a Birmingham church—exposed the dark underside of American democracy. With revolutionary nationalism sweeping Asia and Africa—a movement in which communists often played a prominent role—it was imperative to present a more positive image of American race relations.[5] In 1955, even before the civil rights revolution, Martha Graham's multiracial company (which included black as well as Asian dancers) was sent to Asia in an effort to enhance the image of the United States just as it assumed the colonial mantle of the recently-defeated French in Vietnam.

In the struggle for cultural and political influence in the Third World, nonwhite artists played a pivotal role. Jazz musicians like Louis Armstrong and Duke Ellington were repeatedly sent abroad to help counteract negative publicity about American race relations. The first dance group sponsored under Eisenhower's Emergency Fund was the José Limón Company, dispatched to Brazil and Uruguay in 1954. Like black musicians, black dance companies like Alvin Ailey's were targeted at Africa and Asia (Ailey's first tour was to Japan and Vietnam). But, as Prevots shows, despite the desperate need to counteract negative publicity abroad, the Dance Panel's own artistic standards prevented it from sending black groups overseas before the 1960s. Prevots traces the panel's long, unhappy relationship with Katherine Dunham, who never did get sponsored despite numerous applications and vocal complaints at being spurned, and its reluctance to send Pearl Primus abroad. Numerous factors contributed to the low black representation in the program—the paucity of black-directed companies, the uneven artistic achievements of Dunham and Primus in the 1950s, and the Panel's hostility or indifference to popular forms, such as tap, where black dancers predominated.

Indeed, this question of artistic standards—the politics of dance, as it were—provides the occasion for some of Prevots's most interesting findings. If the panel enthusiastically showcased both ballet and established modern dance companies like Graham's, it proved remarkably hostile to avant-garde dance. In 1955, Merce Cunningham was deemed "too avant-garde and controversial." Only after heated debate was he eventually sent to Europe. Paul Taylor, deemed "avant-garde, but not so much as Merce Cunningham" by one panel member, received sponsorship in 1961. But Alwin Nikolais was rejected as inaccessible and unrepresentative. Reading the minutes of the Dance Panel, one gets the impression that longstanding feuds and different definitions of dance itself had more to do with the choice of artists than Cold War politics.

Notwithstanding its limitations, the touring program offered American dancers a broadening experience, exposure to new audiences, and an indispensable source of income at a time when no other federal support for the arts existed. And, as Prevots points out, in its personnel and its system of review by peer panels, the program strongly influenced the National Endowment for the Arts, established in 1965.

Today, the Cold War is over, and programs of cultural presentation, now under the auspices of the United States Information Agency, have been severely reduced. A related program, by which companies were able to tour the United States, bringing dance to entirely new audiences, was eliminated in the 1980s. As the seemingly unending controversy over the National Endowment for the Arts underscores, the whole idea of government sponsorship of the arts has come under attack. Prevots's careful study reminds us of a time when, whatever the motivation, the government believed that artistic achievement ought to be viewed as one of the glories of American life.

Today, the survival of many artists and arts organizations is threatened. Severe cutbacks in government funding and private support in the last decade have created a crisis in the arts community. In view of the present situation, it is instructive to look back to 1954 when President Dwight D. Eisenhower saw the performing arts not only as an important aspect of American life, but also as a powerful tool in the creation of world peace. He mandated the first public policy and government support for showcasing American dance, music, and theater companies to the rest of the world.

The countries that received our performing artists in the 1950s were stunned—and enthralled. In their eyes we were boorish, uncultured, superficial, and materialistic. We exported movies like *Blackboard Jungle* and sex goddesses like Marilyn Monroe; we exported Elvis Presley with his wiggling hips and hound-dog songs. We sent diplomats abroad whose ignorance of the countries they served bred hostility and mistrust. When William J. Lederer and Eugene Burdick published *The Ugly American* in 1958 excoriating U.S. diplomats in Asia, the title instantly became a household phrase.

In 1948 my father received a Guggenheim Fellowship that took my parents and me to Europe and to Israel that year. I remember going to the movies and seeing nothing but cowboys and Indians. I remember, too, how people everywhere were amazed to find that we read books, went to museums, ate in cheap restaurants, could speak French and Hebrew, and did not own a car. The shock and surprise of how others saw Americans still remains with me.

In the late 1940s and 1950s American politics centered on fears of Communism, its spread both within the U.S. and abroad, and the need for its containment. We were in a fighting mood, locked in struggle with the Soviet Union (our erstwhile ally during World War II), fearful of its ideological and military power, its apparent success in capturing the bodies, minds, and souls of other countries, its willingness to spend millions of dollars on cultural relations, including tours by artists of the highest caliber.

We fought the Communist menace at home as well as abroad. In 1947, the Hollywood Ten were jailed for refusing to "name names" to members of the House Un-American Activities Committee. Beginning in 1950, Senator Joseph R. McCarthy, Republican from Wisconsin, made speeches asserting that dozens of "traitorous" subversives in the government were selling the country out. His wild accusations struck terror in millions of Americans; witch-hunts became the order of the day, creating an environment hostile to dissent. Other countries were seen as dangerously vulnerable to Communist takeover, and to many an arms race seemed the only solution to preserving our economic and political role in the world.

In 1954 Eisenhower took action. He went to Congress, and asked for funds to enlist the performing arts in the Cold War. Thus was born the President's Emergency Fund for International Affairs, which underwrote the nation's first cultural export program geared to the performing arts and sent the José Limón Company—its first dance attraction—to Latin America in 1954. Eisenhower, who as a general had led the Allied troops to victory in World War II, was now practicing "cultural diplomacy," using the arts—rather than bullets, occupying armies, or A-bombs—to win friends and influence policy. The program, a peacetime gamble by a wartime hero, was a resounding success. The media coverage in the countries where American artists performed, the audience attendance as reported in the foreign press, and reports from U.S. foreign service posts all attest to the powerful impression created by American performers wherever they went.

In June 1955, when Eisenhower requested continuance of the Emergency Fund and additional monies for it, hearings were held by a House Subcommittee on Appropriations to review the program. Despite some opposition, the Emergency Fund was confirmed, although there were no additional appropriations. Further congressional hearings were held in 1956 when the Emergency Fund was transformed into permanent legislation. The 1956 hearings are instructive and clearly show changes in attitude among key members of Congress toward the export of American artists. Indeed, the success of the latter as cultural ambassadors helped not only to pass the 1958 bill establishing a National Cultural Center but also to shape the development and organization of the National Endowment for the Arts (NEA), established six years later.

Scholars have questioned whether these American international exchange programs were only thinly disguised vehicles for propaganda. The Central Intelligence Agency (CIA) covertly funded the Congress for Cultural Freedom, which from 1951, shortly after it was founded, until the mid-1960s, when the source of its funding was disclosed, was directed by Nicolas Nabokov, a staunch anti-Communist. Among its accomplishments was the huge Paris arts festival "Masterpieces of the Twentieth Century" that brought dozens of groups, including the Boston Symphony Orchestra and the New York City Ballet, and an exhibition of 150 modern paintings and sculptures to the French capital in 1952. The point was to celebrate the cultural freedom of the West, "draw an inventory," as Nabokov put it, "of [its] achievements in the first fifty years of this century," this at a time when "contemporary art and music were the butts and the victims of...odious repression" in the Soviet Union.[1] Obviously, exposure under these circumstances gave an ideological dimension to the idea of the modern (if not necessarily to the works themselves), a point that both Eva Cockcroft and Serge Guilbaut have made with regard to Abstract Expressionism.[2]

Did something similar occur under the President's Emergency Fund? The answer is no. In dance, as in the other arts, the groups sent abroad were chosen by a panel of professional peers—the model for the peer panels that later became the principal decision-making bodies of NEA. Set up and administered by the American National Theater and Academy (ANTA), these panels not only recommended the artists sent abroad, but also established the policy guidelines to choose them. Through this mechanism, ANTA sought to insulate the selection process from overt political pressure, ensuring that merit would be the chief consideration. As we shall see, the Dance Panel had its disagreements and its prejudices. Its credo was high art, and some of its members had little patience with the avant-garde. Today, we might take umbrage at some of the Panel's ideas and decisions, but it is instructive to see it grappling month after month with issues of artistic quality, professionalism, and representativeness, as well as to see it responding to changes in the society at large, especially at the outset of the 1960s. The story ends in 1962, when the U.S. State Department eliminated ANTA and moved the program, which until then had been based in New York, to Washington, D.C.

As reviews in the foreign press and reports from U.S. diplomats attest, America's image abroad was significantly enhanced by Eisenhower's "Fund." The artists who participated in the program did so not only as performers but also as individuals, whose interactions with citizens of the host country broke down barriers between cultures and ideologies. Paradoxically, the success of American artists abroad enhanced their stature and public recognition at home. International acclaim led to their becoming prophets in their own land. As the twentieth century draws to a close, the history of Eisenhower's "Fund" may provide a powerful argument for support of all our homegrown artists in the millennium to come.

In a letter written on 27 July 1954 to the House Committee on Appropriations, President Dwight D. Eisenhower announced: "I consider it essential that we take immediate and vigorous action to demonstrate the superiority of the products and cultural values of our system of free enterprise." He requested five million dollars "to stimulate the presentation abroad by private firms and groups of the best American industrial and cultural achievements, in order to demonstrate the dedication of the United States to peace and human well-being [and] to offset worldwide Communist propaganda charges that the United States has no culture and that its industrial production is oriented toward war."[1]

The 83rd Congress approved President Eisenhower's request on August 26; Public Law 663 was passed, and thus the President's Emergency Fund for International Affairs came into existence. The Fund was allocated in three categories: the Department of Commerce received $2,592,000 to develop and facilitate U.S. involvement in international trade fairs; the State Department received $2,250,000 for presentations of American dance, theater, music, and sports abroad; finally the United States Information Agency (USIA), which had been created in 1953, was granted $157,000 to help publicize performing arts and sports events.

This was the first time in the history of American public policy that choreographers, composers, playwrights, and their works were systematically funded for export. Indeed, the performing arts, rather than sports, was the chief beneficiary of the $2,250,000 allocation during 1954–1955. The small sum of $83,000 was utilized for sports and various athletic events. Government funding was not meant to pay the full costs of exporting the performing arts. It was expected there would be commercial bookings and private support.

What was it that might have prompted Eisenhower's decision to increase our peacetime visibility through a policy of arts export? Nationally and internationally, the political climate was tense in the 1950s. The Cold War, McCarthyism, violence over civil rights, wars for independence in the Third World, the Korean War, the bomb: these were some of the issues that clouded the American image abroad.

Not long after Eisenhower was sworn in as President in March 1953, Joseph Stalin died in his dacha outside Moscow. His death ushered in the period that novelist Ilya Ehrenburg called "the thaw." The Soviet secret police chief, Lavrenti Beria, was arrested in June, and Georgi Malenkov,

Nikolai Bulganin, Vyacheslav Molotov, along with a then-unknown Nikita S. Khrushchev organized a collective leadership. In a speech to the Supreme Soviet in August 1953, Soviet premier Malenkov talked about "peaceful coexistence." Eisenhower himself, in a speech the previous April to the American Association of Editors, had talked about the possibility of normalizing relations now that Stalin was dead. Stalin's death had also brought about an increase in cultural diplomacy on the part of the Soviet Union; the amount of money spent on sending artists, writers, and performers to other countries escalated considerably.[2]

During the same period of time, America's attention was riveted on the Korean War, which the U.S. had entered in 1950 during Truman's administration. Eisenhower supported the war until October 1952, when he promised, if elected, to end it. The Korean War armistice was signed in July 1953. The key issue at the time was North Korea's insistence on the forced repatriation of approximately 100,000 prisoners of war. On July 27 United Nations and Communist representatives signed an armistice agreement, and North Korea accepted voluntary repatriation of prisoners. Communist China's aid to Korea during the war raised cries for a U.S. blockade of China. Eisenhower refused, calling a blockade an act of war that he was not ready to initiate.

That same year Eisenhower appointed an old friend, Charles Douglas Jackson, as Special Assistant to the President. An executive with Time-Life Publications before and after his one-year appointment, Jackson had been head of psychological warfare in North Africa during World War II. A strong supporter of the arts, he had served on the Metropolitan Opera Board and was instrumental in the development of Lincoln Center.[3]

Jackson's view of psychological warfare was to fight for the minds and souls of the enemy, thus potentially avoiding military combat and destruction. In early 1951, with help from the CIA, he organized the National Committee for a Free Europe. The Committee's chief activity was Radio Free Europe, whose broadcasts to Eastern Europe carried news of freedom and democracy in America as well as anti-Soviet propaganda.

On the first day of August 1953 the United States Information Agency (USIA) came into existence. An independent agency reporting through the National Security Council to the President, the USIA was intended to strengthen American informational and propaganda activities by consolidating a variety of previously existing offices into one institution. C.D. Jackson's interest in psychological warfare had been reinforced by Stalin's death and the Korean armistice. As the President's advisor, Jackson would have encouraged nonmilitary approaches to combating Soviet influence and power.

The mission of the USIA, explained its first director, Theodore C. Streibert, was not "to get foreign people to support the United States, or to sell our ideas abroad." Quite the reverse. "Our mission is to show the peoples of other lands by means of communication techniques...that our objectives and policies are in harmony with and will advance their legitimate aspirations for freedom, progress and peace, meaning that we are trying to identify ourselves with the aims and aspirations of these other people so as to establish a mutuality of interests."[4]

When Eisenhower's Emergency Fund was initiated only a year later, the USIA played an important and key role. An Operations Coordinating Board was established; members included the head of the USIA, the Undersecretaries of State and Defense, representatives from the CIA and the National Security Council, and the Special Assistant to the President (initially Jackson, followed in 1955 by Nelson A. Rockefeller). When artists went abroad under auspices of the Fund, USIA staff on site (known outside the U.S. as USIS) were responsible for coordinating activities and public relations.

There were definitely mixed messages coming from the White House during this period. In September 1953 Eisenhower unveiled his "Atoms for Peace" program, known also as Operation Candor. The basis of the program was that scientific knowledge, particularly atomic energy, could not be confined within national borders forever. Between 1953 and 1956, more than a score of cooperative bilateral atomic research agreements were signed.

At the same time Eisenhower's Secretary of State, John Foster Dulles, made deflecting Communism the cornerstone of his foreign policy. Dulles, historian Martin Walker has written, "would go to almost any length to challenge the Soviet threat."[5] In his 1954 speech to the Council on Foreign Relations, Dulles insisted that "the way to deter aggression is for the free community to be willing and able to respond vigorously at places and with means of its own choosing."[6]

The notion that Communists were everywhere lying in wait to destroy America was given new impetus by Senator Joseph R. McCarthy, in a 1950 speech made in Wheeling, West Virginia. McCarthy explained: "The reason we find ourselves in a position of impotency is...because of the traitorous actions of those who have been treated so well by this Nation....It has not been the less fortunate or members of minority groups who have been selling this nation out, but rather those who have had all the benefits. This is glaringly true in the State Department." He went on to imply that large numbers of individuals working for the government were subversives: "I have in my hand fifty-seven cases of individuals who would appear to be either card-carrying members or certainly loyal to the Communist Party, but who nevertheless are still helping to shape our foreign policy."[7]

The list was a fiction and had been created by the Republican Senator from Wisconsin as an attention-getting scare tactic. "McCarthyism" was launched, bringing with it fear, hatred, and ruined lives. McCarthy wildly pointed fingers, and thousands joined him. Dissent became suspect, and many lost their jobs because they had supported various liberal causes during the 1930s and 1940s. It was known that Eisenhower disliked McCarthy; still he failed to stop him.[8] Finally, on 9 March 1954, the

ABOVE: *President Dwight D. Eisenhower reporting to the nation on the progress of "Operation Alert," a simulated H-bomb attack, from secret headquarters near Washington, D.C., 15 June 1955. Wide World Photos.*

BELOW: *John Foster Dulles, U.S. Secretary of State, at a news conference in 1956 rejecting proposals by the Soviet Union and India that the United States suspend H-bomb tests. UPI/Corbis-Bettmann.*

reporter Edward R. Murrow courageously aired "A Report on Senator Joseph R. McCarthy" on CBS television's *See It Now*. The report provided a powerful review of McCarthy's destructive attacks, unfounded lies, and damaging claims.

Only six weeks later, the Army-McCarthy hearings were held. These were meant to investigate McCarthy's charges that Secretary of the Army Robert T. Stevens and Army Counsel John G. Adams were hampering efforts to uncover Communists in the military. Stevens and Adams countercharged that McCarthy and his assistant Roy Cohn had tried to get preferential treatment for a former staff member, Private G. David Schine. The hearings were carried live on ABC television for nearly two months. The historian David Halberstam would later write: "The nation watched, and when it was over, McCarthy had done himself in with his ugliness."[9]

On July 30 a resolution of censure against McCarthy for conduct unbecoming a Senator was introduced by Senator Ralph E. Flanders, Republican from Vermont. A select committee of the Senate voted to censure McCarthy on two counts. Finally, on December 2, McCarthy was condemned in a special session of the U.S. Senate for his public conduct. When on July 27 Eisenhower had requested funds for peaceful representation of the United States abroad through industrial and cultural exchange, he was certainly mindful of McCarthy's demise as a strong political force. It is somewhat speculative to tie together the Army-McCarthy hearings with the Emergency Fund of 1954, but it could certainly have been a factor encouraging Eisenhower's move in that direction.

RIGHT: *Senator Joseph R. McCarthy. Hank Walker/LIFE Magazine © TIME Inc.*

BELOW: *Soviet premier Nikita S. Khrushchev, flanked by Soviet Foreign Minister Andrei Gromyko (left) and Soviet Defense Minister Rodion Y. Malinovsky, Paris, 1960. National Archives, Washington, D.C.*

McCarthyism did not evaporate with McCarthy's censure. Many on the far right cried out against imagined Communist infiltration of all areas of American society. Not too long after the Symphony of the Air was sent abroad to great acclaim, Congressional hearings were initiated to censure both the artists and the exchange program because of supposed Communist infiltration. Although the orchestra received no further bookings, the climate had changed sufficiently so that the program itself was not harmed.

Just two months following Murrow's television exposé of McCarthy, Chief Justice Earl Warren presided over the unanimous Supreme Court ruling in the case known as *Brown* v. *Board of Education*. "We conclude that in the field of public opinion the doctrine of 'separate but equal' has no place. Separate educational facilities are inherently unequal." This landmark decision, legally ending segregation, marked the beginning of numerous civil rights battles, thus significantly changing political action and public awareness.

Decision-makers on the Dance Panel and in the State Department responded to the events surrounding them. In order to combat criticism of the conflict between democratic ideals and racial iniquities, it was important to send African-American artists abroad under the auspices of

RIGHT: *Federal troops escorting black students to Little Rock Central High School, 1957. Burt Glinn/Magnum Photos, Inc.*

LEFT: *The first Freedom bus burning in Alabama, 1961. Department of Archives and Manuscripts, Birmingham Public Library, Birmingham, Alabama.*

BELOW: *A black protester being arrested in Birmingham, Alabama, 1961. Bruce Davidson/Magnum Photos, Inc.*

Eisenhower's Emergency Fund. Legal desegregation helped pave the way; later, sit-ins and bombings made it even more imperative to seek out and acknowledge African-American artists before the rest of the world.

Support for a production featuring African-American artists came quickly under Eisenhower's Emergency Fund. George Gershwin's musical *Porgy and Bess* toured from December 1954 through February 1955. The world was watching America; how could the government claim racial

"I Have a Dream": Martin Luther King, Jr. delivering his most famous speech at the March on Washington, 1963. Bob Henriques/Magnum Photos, Inc.

equality when they knew about increased civil rights activities? In 1955, Emmett Till, an African-American teenager, was killed in Mississippi for whistling at a white woman; an all-white jury found his murderer not guilty. That same year seamstress Rosa Parks was arrested in Montgomery, Alabama, for not moving to the back of the bus. Governor Orval Eugene Faubus of Arkansas ordered the state National Guard to enforce segregation at Little Rock High School in 1957; Eisenhower responded by sending U.S. Army troops to safeguard entry of nine black students.

In 1960, students from North Carolina A & T College in Greensboro protested segregated dining areas by staging the first "sit-in." In 1963, four young girls were killed by a Ku Klux Klan attack on a Birmingham, Alabama, church; Medgar Wiley Evers, field director for the NAACP in Mississippi, was killed by an unknown assassin outside his own home. Still, there was hope in the air when a quarter-million people marched peacefully on Washington and listened as Martin Luther King, Jr. delivered his "I Have a Dream" speech.

Selma, Alabama, in 1965 was the focus of significant large-scale civil rights activity. On March 7, a group of about 600 began a march from Selma to Montgomery, protesting segregation and a lack of voting rights for African-Americans. They never made it to Montgomery; Alabama state troopers struck the marchers with clubs and fired tear gas canisters into the crowd. On March 9, a group of whites attacked three ministers from Boston who had come to Selma for the march. One of them, the Reverend James J. Reeb, was hit in the head with a pipe and died two days later. A third march from Selma to Montgomery started on March 21; 3,200 black and white marchers began the fifty-four mile journey under the protection of 4,000 Alabama National Guard troops mobilized by President Lyndon B. Johnson. On March 25 the march ended peacefully, but that evening two civil rights workers were attacked by a Ku Klux Klan group, and one of them died instantly. The events in Selma helped speed the passage of the Voting Rights Act, signed into law by President Lyndon B. Johnson on 6 August 1965.

It would appear that the export of some of our best African-American artists in fairly substantial numbers was directly related to the tremendous amount of civil rights activity in the 1950s and 1960s. Even Lincoln Kirstein, General Manager for the New York City Ballet and dance panelist for Eisenhower's Fund, participated in the 1965 Selma marches. Subsequently, he wrote a moving poem in commemoration of the events. During the period 1955–1965, the African-American artists and attractions that received State Department sponsorship for one, if not several tours abroad, included *Porgy and Bess*, the Jubilee Singers, Marian Anderson, Louis Armstrong, Dizzie Gillespie, William Warfield, Camilla Williams, the Alvin Ailey dance company, and the Howard University Choir.

Eisenhower's Emergency Fund was also shaped by a long history of private involvement in cultural and educational exchange—what we know now as cultural diplomacy. At the beginning of the twentieth century, Andrew Carnegie took the position that the exchange of ideas and individuals could be an important factor in eliminating conflict between nations. In keeping with the American idea that private initiative rather than government control was the path to follow, he created in 1919 the Carnegie Endowment for International Peace. The emphasis was on sponsoring exchanges of professors, students, and publications, stimulating translations and the book trade, and encouraging the teaching of English. Much of the activity was aimed at Latin America with the idea of spreading knowledge about us as a neighbor, thus fostering friendly relations.

Two other private initiatives date from the early decades of the twentieth century. The Rockefeller Foundation, established in 1913, became involved in cultural exchange during the 1920s. The International Institute of Education, founded in 1919 to achieve peace through international understanding, focused primarily on student exchange. These early efforts in cultural diplomacy were characterized by Frank Ninkovitch as "a form of statecraft concerned with the management of intellectual influences on international politics."[10] They reflected a belief in volunteerism and the avoidance of government control to spread the values of moral rearmament. The emphasis was not so much on putting forward the idea of the superiority of American capitalism or our particular way of life, but rather the premise that leaders could institute a meeting of the minds that would avoid and prevent misunderstandings by many in the political, educational, and artistic arenas.

The late 1930s saw an increase in anti-American propaganda in Latin

America on the part of both the Communists and the Axis powers. Private exchange efforts were no longer considered sufficient. In 1938 a Division of Cultural Affairs was established within the State Department; it was headed by Dr. Ben Cherrington, who had been associated with the University of Denver as director of its Foundation for the Advancement of Social Science. The mandate of this new Division was to create public/private partnerships in Latin American exchange programs.

In 1940, with Europe now caught up in World War II (which the U.S. would enter the following year), President Franklin D. Roosevelt saw the need for stronger government involvement in Latin America. A new agency was created, headed by Nelson A. Rockefeller; his official title was Coordinator of Inter-American Affairs (CIAA). He was charged with developing short-term exchange initiatives, as opposed to long-range projects planned by the Division of Cultural Affairs. Major projects for both Rockefeller and Cherrington involved student and teacher exchange, the transmission of specially created radio broadcasts, the development of educational motion pictures, and the exchange of books and publications. In 1946, a year after hostilities ended, Rockefeller's office was eliminated; it had been a wartime measure and was no longer deemed necessary.

One of Rockefeller's early projects was in the field of dance. In 1941 he approached his friend Lincoln Kirstein about sending a ballet company on a goodwill tour of Latin America. The government would agree to underwrite all operating expenses of the tour if Kirstein would take care of production costs. The dancers were recruited from Kirstein's defunct Ballet Caravan, choreographer George Balanchine's defunct American Ballet, and advanced students from the School of American Ballet. The new company, American Ballet Caravan, was directed by Balanchine. According to J. Manuel Espinosa the tour cost $100,000 and lasted twenty-eight weeks.[11] It was for this tour that Balanchine choreographed two of his greatest works, *Ballet Imperial* and *Concerto Barocco*. Bernard Taper, in his biography of Balanchine, explains: "The aim of the project was to reveal to the people of South America, through a medium that transcended the language barrier, that the North American colossus had a soul and was not just a grasping materialist."[12]

Between 1946 and 1948, two important pieces of legislation were signed into law that furthered the cause of cultural diplomacy by emphasizing exchanges of individuals and educational materials. These were the Fulbright and the Smith-Mundt Acts. Neither of these two Acts established policy concerning the export of American performing artists and attractions, but they were important milestones in government sponsorship of international exchange.[13]

On 1 August 1946, the Fulbright Act was signed into law by President Truman. It did not go into effect until November 1947, when the first of the bilateral agreements it called for was signed with China. According to Fulbright's plan, a portion of the payments made by foreign governments in their own currency to the United States for the purchase of surplus war property was to be used in the case of each country to finance educational exchange between that country and the United States. The first Fulbright scholars went to China in 1948, and soon Fulbright scholars became a key element in our educational exchange policy.[14]

The Fulbright Act reflected Senator Fulbright's personal experience as a Rhodes scholar at Oxford and his belief that understanding between countries was encouraged by the association of individuals and institutions. Fulbright fellowships for teachers and scholars are still a major force in cultural diplomacy.

In January 1948 the Smith-Mundt Act was passed. It was administered by the Office of International Information and the Office of Educational Exchange. The Office of International Information had a mandate to make available overseas information about our policies and all matters affecting foreign affairs. The mandate for the Office of Educational Exchange was to create cooperative ventures with other nations in the interchange of persons, knowledge, and skills, the rendering of technical and other services, and the interchange of developments in the field of education, the arts, and sciences.

After World War II, Germany became the focus of a significant effort in cultural diplomacy. Two Berlin cultural festivals, in 1951 and 1952, were funded by the American government. Henry J. Kellerman, who was responsible for formulating State Department policy and overseeing cultural affairs with Germany from 1945 to 1949, explained the rationale for the festivals:

> The break between the United States intellectual community and Germany in the thirties was radical and complete. With few exceptions the postwar effort to restore the broken ties started from point zero.... In the case of the policy pursued by the United States in occupied Germany, it was conceived and designed more sharply than any other program as an instrument of foreign policy.... It was an integral part of the total military, political and economic operation.[15]

The 1951 Berlin Cultural Festival took place during the month of September and included a fairly wide range of American performing artists and attractions. Singers included soprano Astrid Varnay, who appeared as a guest artist in *Tristan and Isolde*, and the Hall Johnson Choir. A production of *Medea* featured Judith Anderson. The musical *Oklahoma!*, the Juilliard String Quartet, and the dance-mime Angna Enters were other American contributions to the Festival. Kellerman's report continued: "The idea underlying this singular undertaking was to demonstrate the high standards of American performing arts achievements and, by implication, to refute Nazi and Communist propaganda clichés of American cultural insensibility and sterility."[16]

The New York City Ballet opened the 1952 Berlin Cultural Festival to rave reviews. *Die Neue Zeitung* wrote on September 5: "One can dream of nothing more uniform and more balanced than this well-disciplined team from New York."[17] Four days later, a reviewer in the same newspaper observed: "The last performance of the New York City Ballet again showed the versatility and high quality of the ensemble. All the soloists as well as the ensemble were welcomed enthusiastically by the Berlin public." On September 5 *Der Tagesspiegel* noted that "the Berlin public [had] received its guests from New York with hearty enthusiasm." The day before, *Nacht Depesche* had described the company as a pleasure to behold.

Other participants in the 1952 Berlin Cultural Festival were singers Polyna Stoska and Kenneth Spencer, pianist Alexander Brailowsky, and the touring company of *Porgy and Bess*. Kellerman was delighted with the results, all the more so because his ideas had not met with unanimous applause. He wrote:

> The success of the American presence (1952) was nothing short of spectacular. The author decided to send Gershwin's "Porgy and Bess" to the festival from whence it was to go to other European capitals. Well-meaning friends advised against it. So did prominent members of the American black community, who feared that German or even any European audiences were not ready to appreciate the message and that the sordid misery of Catfish Alley would be taken to portray the normal life of the American black community. Yet the performance of a 65 all-black member cast was a triumph. It literally overwhelmed the Berlin audience. Comments in West Berlin were lyrical and not one critical note was heard from the Communist press in East Berlin.[18]

Several State Department reports were written about the Berlin Cultural Festivals, many of which expressed criticism about lack of sufficient time for planning, excessive admission charges, too many events in too short a time period, insufficient budget, and poor performance facilities. One report recommended that the festivals be continued, but extended over a longer period of time, and that American performing arts should be scheduled all year round:

> The countries of Western Europe habitually consider their cultural history, current cultural events and prestige, of far greater importance than we do. This report should be read against a background of several…reports which describe the emphasis and the method of approach to the German mind which the Soviets have employed in several cultural fields since they captured Berlin. . . . It should be recalled that within two weeks after the fall of Berlin, the Soviet authorities were busily engaged in locating theater costumes and music scores to reopen theaters for thoughtful audiences made up of their recent enemy….It is significant that the Soviet controlled press had no answer to the highly laudatory press accounts of the press in the Western Sector of Berlin. Its silence was audible….The endless Soviet-inspired attacks and supplementary innuendos concerning cultural immaturity are directed against the United States and not against Great Britain or France.[19]

This report urged that we continue "American participation in cultural events" not just in Germany, but all over Europe. In April 1953 President Eisenhower signed an agreement to "continue within the limits of available funds, a program of cultural assistance to Germany."[20] The success of our performing arts activities in that country certainly must have made an impact on the President; it was only one year later that he asked for money to fund American cultural exports all over the world.

At the July 1955 Geneva Foreign Ministers meeting, a seventeen-point proposal was submitted to the Soviet Union by the United States, France, and the United Kingdom. The first item on the list proposed that freer exchange of information and ideas should be facilitated. Other suggestions included exchange of books, periodicals, and newspapers; exchange of exhibitions; and cultural and sports exchanges—all on a reciprocal basis.

Although Foreign Minister Molotov rejected the initiative, he indicated a willingness to entertain bilateral or multilateral agreements that might reflect the interests of the different countries concerned. The performances by the Moiseyev Dance Company in Paris and London that year were an outgrowth of the Geneva talks. In October and November, pianist Emil Gilels and violinist David Oistrakh were the first Soviet artists in several decades to appear in the United States. The next year, American impresario Sol Hurok arranged Soviet tours for violinist Isaac Stern and singer Jan Peerce. He also went to the Soviet Union and began negotiating for an American tour of the Moiseyev Dance Company; it eventually came in 1958.

Dance was certainly high on the list of successful cultural exports in all directions. London reviews praised the Moiseyev's 1955 performances in glowing terms. Paul Tassovin wrote in his London notebook for *Dance Observer*: "The Igor Moiseyev Ensemble from Moscow exploded in London this November like an A-Bomb."[21] Joan Lawson, calling the group the "Moscow State Folk Dancers," wrote in *The Dancing Times* : "Bursting on to the stage like flames through an autumn bonfire, these dancers pour out their infectious energy."[22]

Eisenhower's 1954 Emergency Fund launched American dance exports all over the world. Soviet interest in sending the Moiseyev company in 1958 and the Bolshoi Ballet in 1959 was a response to their exposure to American dance at the Berlin Festivals and, later, in other countries and cities. American interest in high quality dance exports was a source both of competition and pride.

The orchestra applauded us, after which the first violinist stood up and, in the best English at his command, stated that he and the rest of the members wanted us to know that it was their honor to be playing for a company of artists. We had won our first step towards accomplishing our mission.[1]

These words were written by a member of the José Limón Company, the first dance group funded under Eisenhower's new Emergency Fund. Its performances in November and December 1954 received rave reviews from critics in Rio de Janeiro, São Paulo, and Montevideo. The American Embassy sent a message to the State Department: "Limón Company top artistic and personal success. Even writer unfriendly United States praised highly."[2] Eisenhower's mission of reaching other people through our performing arts had been launched!

The program was initiated with a request to the State Department in the fall of 1954. Many other countries were sending performing groups to the conference of the Inter-American Economic and Social Council in Rio de Janeiro, and the UNESCO conference that would shortly follow in Montevideo. The State Department deemed it extremely important that the United States have a strong presence through representative American culture. The USIA made its objectives regarding Latin America clear in a 1955 statement:

> The strategic importance of Latin America and the size of our stake in that area are well known. What is not so well known is that, first, a tremendous social and economic change, an upsurge, is taking place throughout Latin America; and, second, international communism is systematically exploiting the problems arising from that upsurge, seeking to foment hatred of the United States and establish footholds in the hemisphere.[3]

One factor in the choice of José Limón was that he was Mexican-born and Spanish-speaking. John Martin, the dance critic of *The New York Times*, commented on this in a review of the tour, which he accompanied:

> To send a Mexican-born dancer with a Spanish name into the Southern continent may look, at a quick glance, like a sure thing. But Mr. Limón himself saw in advance that just the reverse was the case for him, and he had hardly put foot on foreign soil before he began his campaign of correction. Though he spoke Spanish, which was a great help, he announced

loudly and firmly that he knew nothing of the Spanish dance, and could not do a zapateado or a farucca if his life depended on it. Indeed, he could not even do a jarabe, for he left Mexico in infancy, was educated in North America, thought like a North American, and worked in the so-called modern dance, which had come to life in North America and was one of the most thoroughly indigenous art forms.[4]

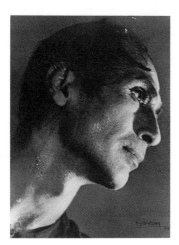

José Limón, Rio de Janeiro, 1954. Photo by F. Pamplona. Dance Collection, The New York Public Library for the Performing Arts, Astor, Lenox, and Tilden Foundations.

Pauline Koner, one of the company's leading dancers, reminisced in *Solitary Song* that Limón "was particularly happy that South America as well as Mexico had now accepted him, and the fact that he spoke Spanish brought him close to the people and the press."[5] Limón's fluency in Spanish helped the audience achieve greater understanding of the originality and value of American modern dance. He told audiences in Rio and Montevideo: "With all our crudities, we are Americans. We are not afraid to declare ourselves, and have done so in our dance. The academic dance from Europe is not adequate to express what we have to say. Hemingway and Faulkner write in English, but they write like Americans. In the same way, we are trying to find a new language for American Dance."[6]

Language was, of course, not the only reason for choosing Limón. In 1954 he was considered one of the most important modern dance choreographers. Forty-six years old, he was in his prime as a creator, performer, and teacher. His mentor was Doris Humphrey, who, along with Martha Graham, had been a major figure in the creative transformation of American modern dance. While Limón did not create a new movement vocabulary as Humphrey and Graham had, his choreography was beautifully crafted, deeply expressive, and original.

By 1954 Limón had created two masterpieces, and both were performed on the tour. *The Moor's Pavane*, choreographed in 1949, was one of the first modern dance works to enter the ballet repertory. The story was based on *Othello*, Shakespeare's great play of love, jealousy and revenge, power and race, which Limón had distilled with consummate skill. Another work, *La Malinche*, also created in 1949, was set in Mexico at the time of the sixteenth-century Spanish invasion; it was the story of an Aztec princess torn between her love of country and her love for a Spanish conquistador. In addition to Limón's own choreography, his company performed works by Doris Humphrey, including the exhilarating *Variations and Conclusions* from *New Dance*. Another Humphrey work in the repertory was the mysterious *Night Spell*, in which a dreamer struggles with three disturbing creatures of his fantasy. The dance begins in an atmosphere of darkness and gloom, with images of falling and flight; at the end the dreamer finds hope in the embrace of one of the night's disappearing phantoms. In addition to these four works, the tour repertory

RIGHT: *Doris Humphrey as the Matriarch in* With My Red Fires, *1938. Photo by Barbara Morgan. Barbara Morgan Archives.*

BELOW: *José Limón as the Moor in* The Moor's Pavane, *1949. Photo by Walter Strate. Dance Collection, The New York Public Library for the Performing Arts, Astor, Lenox, and Tilden Foundations.*

included Limón's *Vivaldi Concerto*, an early work, and Humphrey's *Day on Earth*, *Ritmo Jondo*, *Ruins and Visions*, and *Story of Mankind*.

The José Limón Company arrived in Rio de Janeiro on 22 November 1954 and went to São Paulo on November 30. The next stop was Montevideo, where the group performed from December 7–10 at the Teatro Solis. Pauline Koner called this a "lovely old-world theater" and noted that evening performances began at ten o'clock:

> Trying to whip up performance pitch so late was a trial, but we knew we had a unique audience—sophisticated, international. It was culturally and politically important to make a strong impression. This was the climax of our trip. The advance press and reviews were exceptional and the audiences enthusiastic. After the opening night performance, the American delegation came back stage to congratulate us.... I could see the faces beaming with enthusiasm and relief. Montevideo really took us to its heart. Ten o'clock performances suddenly became a pleasure.[7]

When Eisenhower requested additional monies for the renewal of his Emergency Fund in 1955, the company's expenses were scrutinized by a subcommittee of the House Appropriations Committee. Representative Prince H. Preston, Democrat from Georgia, was among those who doubted that the tour had been handled wisely: "It certainly appears to me that you have a mighty loose way of handling the taxpayer's dollars. I will say, in fairness to the troupe, that they did a very fine job in Montevideo, and it was quite impressive to the large number of delegates who were there from all over the world. I thought it was a splendid show."[8]

These June 1955 hearings revealed not only profound ignorance about the arts but also active hostility toward them on the part of many congressmen. The hearings were chaired by Representative John James Rooney, Democrat from New York.[9] In his opening statement, Acting Secretary of State Herbert Hoover, Jr. attempted to convey the value of the program:

> The Department is, of course, vitally interested in all phases of the program, touching, as it does, on many aspects of our foreign policy. There have been many shifts and changes in the Cold War during the last year.... We must of course remain vigilant.... No matter what progress will be achieved, there will be fundamental and basic differences between the ideologies of the free world and the Communist systems. Greater and greater emphasis may well fall on the economic and cultural differences between the two conflicting systems.... The promotion of peaceful United States objectives should be facilitated by every means at our disposal. Frequently, an international trade fair, an important cultural event, or a scientific gathering provide opportunities to influence public sentiment, of value as great, or even greater, than more formal official occasions.

The total cost of the Limón tour was $35,400, and the Congressmen reviewed every single expenditure. They found it hard to comprehend what a dance company was, how it toured, what it needed, and why so many precious tax dollars were necessary to keep it going. It was noted by Representative Rooney that the budget broke down into four items: $410 for getting the scenery and costumes in order; $22,658 for international transportation of persons, scenery, and costumes; $11,427 as reimbursement of losses to a South American impresario; and $905 as a cancellation fee to the Brooklyn Academy of Music.

The first budget item challenged by the subcommittee was the $410 for costumes and scenery. Julius F. Seebach, testifying on behalf of USIA, explained that the costumes had to be cleaned and the scenery assembled. Congressman Rooney asked, "What happened to the scenery and costumes after you spent $410 on them? Whose property were they by then?"

The next item questioned was the $905 cancellation reimbursement. Seebach explained: "One of the important members of the cast had an engagement at the Brooklyn Academy of Music, and had been advertised and had agreed to appear. In order to get the manager of the Brooklyn Academy of Music to release this person, it was necessary to make up to him for his loss of the expenditures which he had already made." Rooney then moved on to the next budget item of $11,427 to reimburse the company's South American impresario:

> MR. SEEBACH. As to the reimbursement of the loss of the South American impresario, there were two factors that controlled this: one was that it was rather deep into the spring, or really into the summer, in South America, when their theatrical season was at its low point of the year, and secondly, that they would not have enough time to promote and exploit these performances, so as to get the largest possible audiences. The result of it is that the income was lower by that amount than had been anticipated. Normally, under a normal contract, . . . this would be the attraction's own problem. We had, because of these two conferences, more or less insisted that these impresarios put on these performances.
>
> MR. ROONEY. Is that your explanation of an expenditure of $11,427 of the taxpayers' money?
>
> MR. SEEBACH. Yes, sir.
>
> MR. ROONEY. Who is the South American impresario?
>
> MR. SEEBACH. Mr. Hawkins, do you have his name?
>
> MR. ROONEY. While you are at it, please tell us exactly what an impresario is.

Rooney requested that an itemized list of expenditures by the impresario be submitted for the record. He asked to see box office receipts of $7,801.55 for the fourteen performances; receipts for $6,937.92 in expenses and $12,181.63 in payments to the company; for audit fees of $102 and even a bank service charge of $7.72. This attention to the most minute details of the tour was really a way for officials like Rooney to register their opposition to government funding of artistic activity as well as question the value of overseas exchanges.

By the time the June 1955 congressional hearings took place, *Porgy and Bess* had already completed a hugely succesful tour under the auspices of Eisenhower's program. A collaboration of composer George Gershwin, dramatist DuBose Heyward, and librettist Ira Gershwin, *Porgy and Bess* premiered in 1935 and was first revived in 1942. The revival that toured abroad in the 1950s was directed by Robert Breen; it had premiered in June 1952 and played in four U.S. cities—Dallas, Chicago, Pittsburgh, and Washington—before leaving for Europe. Its appearance at the Berlin Festival in 1952 was under government auspices; however, its other performances that year and its appearances the following year in London and Paris were commercial ventures.

The State Department was interested in reaching audiences in Eastern Europe, the Middle East, and areas in Western Europe where economic conditions had in the past prevented American performing artists from touring. Breen had lost money with the production even in cities with well-functioning theaters, ready-made audiences, good impresarios, and decent public relations mechanisms. In December 1954, under the auspices of the Emergency Fund, *Porgy and Bess* began a three-month tour that took the production to Zagreb, Belgrade, Alexandria, Cairo, Naples, Milan, Athens, Tel Aviv, Casablanca, and Barcelona.

A *New York Times* story, filed from Yugloslavia at the start of the tour, lauded the *Porgy and Bess* company for its accomplishments offstage as well as onstage:

> All of Yugoslavia is singing today. The workers and the peasants are singing. The communist officials, the man in the street, the students, all are singing the songs of George Gershwin and the praises of the cast of the folk opera *Porgy and Bess....* All of the warm emotion of the Slav character welled up in a joyous affection for the seventy Negroes who came here a week ago and did more than put on shows in Zagreb and Belgrade. They made America and her people better known and appreciated. And the United States Government, itself, shared in Yugoslavia thanks for making it possible, reaping more expressions of gratitude than ever were extended for military and economic aid here. Devoid of crude propaganda efforts, the presentation of life on Catfish Row startled Yugoslavs with its honesty. They responded, as one government official put it, 'with the observation that only psychologically mature people could have placed this on stage.' With charm and grace, members of the cast created new perspectives here for a Communist-led people sensitive to reports of American race prejudice and discrimination. These were conveyed through an extraordinary number of offstage personal contacts. Artists showed themselves everywhere, on streets, in places of entertainment, hotels and in private homes, where many questions were bluntly asked and honestly answered.[10]

At the famous La Scala Opera House in Milan, the manager was quoted as saying: "Tomorrow...I will be acclaimed either an idiot or a genius." As it turned out, all eight performances of *Porgy and Bess* at La Scala were sold out, and the management wanted the troupe to stay for another week. There were reports of fourteen to twenty curtain calls. Richard Coe, a Washington drama critic, commented on the musical's success, noting that the Milanese typically "look with some dismay on the United States of America as being strong, perhaps, but somehow barbaric, insensitive and juvenile at best."[11]

On their last day in Cairo, the cast of *Porgy* was summoned to receive Egyptian President Nasser's personal expression of appreciation; one journalist wrote: "If this is propaganda, let us have more of it."[12] In Tel Aviv, the demand for seats was so great that on the day of the last performance 200 desperate fans crashed through a window of the theater and took up stations in vacant spots in the aisles and in the wings. An amusing anecdote from a tour report gives the flavor of the tour's impact in Israel:

> In Tel Aviv—at Ambassador Lawson's reception for the Company—the Russian Ambassador said, with gleaming face to Mrs. Ira Gershwin, "Oh—if only WE had a PORGY AND BESS—WE—would—send—it!" and then he wound up with an "oh!" and a global gesture. It is impossible to transmit on paper the knowing intent of his gesture.[13]

The 1955 hearings treated *Porgy and Bess* a good deal more gently than the Limón tour, although the summary indicated a pervasive hostility to arts exchange in general. After finding that the eleven weeks of performances had cost the government $285,000, Representative Frank T. Bow, Republican from Ohio, decided to ask a series of questions. Robinson McIlvaine, Deputy Assistant Secretary for Public Affairs in the Department of State, was the individual who chaired the interagency committee that authorized payments. Bow addressed his questions to McIlvaine:

> MR. BOW. Just what do you pay them as travel expenses?
>
> MR. MCILVAINE. I can give you that. The operating expenses are $17,735.66.
>
> MR. BOW. How is that broken down?
>
> MR. MCILVAINE. That is in salaries.
>
> MR. BOW. In other words, you pay them salaries?
>
> MR. MCILVAINE. No; we do not pay salaries.
>
> MR. BOW. That is what I am trying to find out, and if you will give us that information, we will appreciate it. What have you actually paid, and what part of it do you pay?
>
> MR. MCILVAINE. We pay the difference between what they take in and what keeps them from going broke, in effect.
>
> MR. BOW. Are there any profits paid to their booking agents?

MR. McILVAINE. There are no profits, other than whatever fees there are. There are salaries for the actors, and salaries for everyone who is involved. Now, whether you call that a profit or not, I do not think you would....I think this question of profits with these organizations is a tough one. Mr. Davis has around $225,000 I believe, of his own money in this thing, to which he has said "goodby." I do not think there is much profit in it for anyone. We hope that the actors are able to make their salaries, and that is about it.

Representative Rooney continued the questioning. He turned to Representative Cliff Clevenger, Republican from Ohio, to inquire if that gentleman had any further questions. The response indicated distaste with the notion of spending any government money on the arts or paying to send performers abroad.

MR. ROONEY. Mr. Clevenger, do you have any questions?

MR. CLEVENGER. Mr. Chairman, I have no questions. We are operating in a field where I am not willing to operate at all. When we are running a deficit of probably $3,500 million this year....I wonder where in the Constitution you can find anything that gives me the right to spend the taxpayers' money for projects of this sort....National defense costs for the military alone are running $33 billion, or $34 billion a year, and in view of that situation, how many of these frills can I vote for?...We go on the defensive immediately when some propagandist connected with people whose ideologies are different from ours charges us with having no culture. The world knows better....Just how responsible are we as representatives of the people when we vote to continue this madness until the crash takes us over? I just simply cannot find the justification to take it away from the people. I am out of sympathy with it.

The third largest performing arts group to be exported under the aegis of the Emergency Fund in 1955 was the Symphony of the Air. This orchestra, which NBC had formerly sponsored with Arturo Toscanini as conductor, had just become a free-lance organization. The orchestra was playing under the direction of the tour's guest conductors—Thor Johnson of the Cincinnati Orchestra, Walter Hendl of the Dallas Symphony, and Nicolas Moldavan, a violist with Symphony of the Air. From May 3 through June 25 the orchestra toured East Asia. Its intensive schedule included performances in Tokyo, Nagoya, Takarazuka, Kyoto, Hiroshima, Fukuoka, Sendai, Yokohama and Shizuoka, Japan; Seoul, Korea; Taipei, Taiwan; Manila, Philippines; Bangkok, Thailand; Kuala Lumpur, Malaysia; and Colombo, Ceylon. Two primary concerns motivated this intense musical penetration of the Far East: State Department paranoia about Communist influence in these countries and the limited number of American performing arts presentations in the region. According to testimony given at the 1955 congressional hearing, no Western orchestra had ever visited Japan before.

The reports presented at the June 1955 hearings about the Symphony of the Air tour were glowing. When the orchestra played in Tokyo, lines of students—the estimates ran as high as eight thousand—had camped outside the box office, playing cards, drinking tea, and singing songs throughout the night. The orchestra arranged an extra student performance because of a petition signed by three thousand students who were unable to get tickets. While the students waited in line, members of the orchestra came by and talked with them. Paul Renzi, Jr. wrote in the *Musical Courier*:

> Many of the musicians stayed with the line and talked with the students, brought them refreshments and even shared their blankets until the box office opened at nine the following morning. Some of us cried like babies afterward. It was an experience that none of us will ever forget.... They are the future leaders of Japan.... They are extremely enthusiastic about the arts and sciences.... One United States representative has informed us that our music and our individual activities and attitudes have done more towards establishing a close rapport between our countries than a staff of attachés could hope to do in years.

The Japanese newspapers devoted long articles to the orchestra's visit. A writer in the English-language edition of *Osaka Mainchi* wrote: "As the symphony was brought to the grand finale, the crowds who sat in an ecstasy of tonal splendor knew no end of jolly." In another Japanese city a newspaper reported: "Members of the audience forgot for the moment their social status.... They forgot their nationalities and racial differences.... Music is really an excellent bridge to transport the friendly feelings of nations.

Cables and reports, sent by the American Embassy, transmitted news of the orchestra's remarkable reception. On May 4: "Symphony of the Air opening performances last night outstanding success. Orchestra played to Crown Prince, other members of Imperial household, prominent Japanese government, industrial and cultural leaders; Diplomatic Corps in Tokyo well represented by several Ambassadors. Ranking American Embassy officers from Ambassador down also in attendance, many with small parties of influential Japanese." From Japan the orchestra went to Korea and in Seoul 13,000 people attended a concert on the grounds of the capital. A report noted: "The triumphs that had been enjoyed in Japan were repeated. There was the same eagerness to come more closely in touch with Americans and American thought and life."

The orchestra's tour was still in progress during the Emergency Fund hearings, which were held from June 13 to June 20; this may be why it escaped close scrutiny at that time. In fact, much of the hearing was devoted to testimony in favor of the Fund presented by a representative of William Randolph Hearst, who was in Europe on a business trip and could not attend.

Speaking on Hearst's behalf was Frank Coniff, one of his editorial assistants. The core of Coniff's testimony was based on a series of articles that had appeared in the Hearst newspapers. These were written during the week of February 13 when Prime Minister Georgi Malenkov was forced to resign in a power play with Nikita S. Khrushchev, who assumed control as Secretary General of the Communist Party. In one article Hearst himself wrote:

> The Soviet Union can't stand war with the West within the foreseeable future and therefore won't start one.... The democracies won't start war with the Soviet Union because it is against the very nature of democracy to launch an aggressive war.... If I am right in thinking that war is no solution to the current struggle and that Russia will not pull the trigger for varying reasons, then we pass into the much more difficult battleground of peace. The West is well equipped in any trial on arms. But are we prepared practically and philosophically to surpass Communism in the thornier problems of peace?

Hearst felt that the "cold war...is going to be much more subtle than it was under Stalin." The phrase used by Coniff during the congressional hearings to describe what he and Hearst thought was needed was "competitive coexistence." This meant that the United States would have to find ways of revealing the American way of life to the people of the Soviet Union and the Communist bloc countries, while demonstrating an openness to the peoples and cultures of different countries. Coniff commented: "We just came back from Russia so full of the belief that the American way of life has so much more to offer than the Russian way of life that if we can let the people of the world see it, believe me, any comparison is bound to tip the balance in our favor."

According to Coniff, it was not the military front that was important to the Soviets, but the ideological one:

> We did gain the impression that they had the idea that in the coming years they could so manipulate events that they would gain an edge on us in this cold war, which I now think is a soft war.... In accordance to their own theory, the Russians seem to feel that every form of endeavor is subject to ideological struggle, and such a thing like sports and the theater and an avenue like literature are weapons to the Russians in this struggle with us.

In the same testimony, Coniff went on to support the idea that cultural ventures had an important role to play in future relations with the Soviet Union. "It is the impression of Mr. Hearst and Mr. Kingsbury Smith and myself that our American artists can help also in winning opinions among our allies, among the uncommitted nations, and even back of the Iron Curtain we can do a lot to dispel the thought that America is concerned only with material things. Some headway has already been made in that."

Toward the end of the June 1955 hearings, a Washington, D.C. impresario, Patrick Hayes, told a story demonstrating how art could change the national image and yield concrete military and political gains:

It seems that each year our government must negotiate with the Government of Iceland for the air bases we maintain there. It is always done on a year to year basis and some Icelanders are not in favor of military bases in their peaceful country, so the negotiations are a matter of routine. Each year the Russians do all they can to hamper the negotiations, and in particular play on the theme that Americans are militaristic and materialistic, in contrast to the cultural and peaceful characteristics of Icelanders, and of course, as they put it, the Russians themselves. Congressman Kearns was a member of the negotiating team, and he arranged for the United States Air Force Band and Orchestra to stop in Iceland for a visit on its way to Europe. At one of the concerts, Kearns took the baton and led the orchestra. This had never happened in Iceland before, a legislator qualified to conduct a symphony orchestra....Kearns was a musician before being a Congressman. The result was a near sensation not only in the applause that greeted the performance, but in the impact on the Icelanders. Kearns and his colleagues from America, were regarded in a new light from that moment forward, and the negotiations were smooth and swift. Kearns credits a musical performance with a major assist in our international relations.

As a result of the hearings, Congress agreed to Eisenhower's request for an extension of the Emergency Fund, but he was denied additional monies. The program may have been successful, but neither Representatives Rooney, Clevenger, and Prince, nor the many conservatives in Congress would be swayed. Before long Rooney attacked the program with even greater force.

In March 1956, at another hearing before the Subcommittee of the Committee on Appropriations, Rooney brought forward charges against the Symphony of the Air. The record makes for chilling reading. In an attempt to smear the entire arts exchange program, he asserted that several members of the Symphony of the Air were Communists or Communist sympathizers, and that taxpayer money was being spent on dangerous and subversive activities.

Rooney had managed to get Dennis A. Flinn from the Office of Security to check the backgrounds of orchestra members to determine if any past or present Communist affiliations existed. The implication was that artists could be dangerous; if supported under Eisenhower's Fund, the potential existed of their supporting subversive activity abroad. Although it was evident that Rooney had no clear proof of such activity on the part of orchestra members, he kept trying to establish guilt:

Mr. Rooney. On or about the 18 of January 1956, were you in touch with me, Mr. Flinn?

Mr. Flinn. That is correct.

Mr. Rooney. At that time I told you that I had the name of a certain person in the city of New York which had been sent to me by a retired detective of the police department of that city...including the name and address and telephone number of the informant?

MR. FLINN. That is correct.

MR. ROONEY. And what did you then do?

MR. FLINN. I referred it to the FBI....They reported the interview with the original informant named in the letter to you.

MR. ROONEY. Let us stay with the original informant....We will call him No. 6....What did No. 6 say?

MR. FLINN. He identified himself as associated with this orchestra in the past, and stated that since the last election of officers of the orchestra, when the leftist groups took control, he has not played with the orchestra....He attributed his lack of further employment to an incident that took place in 1955 when the arrangements were made for the trip to the Orient. He made the comment that some of the fellows were going to have difficulty in making the tour because they would have difficulty in getting a passport because of their background. Since that statement...he was constantly watched by the "leftists"....He said...that No. 8 highly praised and agreed with a book which condemned the atom bombing of Hiroshima....No. 9...constantly praised Russian music....He admitted that he could not be specific as to the allegations of the Red propaganda, nor cite specific instances as to the spread of the propaganda. He did furnish, however, a list of 30 individuals suspected by him of being "leftists." This informant was also not quite articulate when asked to define the term "leftist."

MR. ROONEY. Did he not say that he believed there were certain people who were un-American?

MR. FLINN. Un-American; yes.

MR. ROONEY. What did No. 36 say?

MR. FLINN. He said that he had no special information regarding the spread of Red propaganda, but felt and had heard that several members of the orchestra were Communists....[H]e felt that a certain local union is controlled by the Communist faction...[and that] because of his own rightist tendencies...he had been held back in his career in the music profession....No. 7...was registered with the American Labor Party, 1937 and 1938; 1940–44; and 1946, 1948–52. In addition there is reference to the fact that he was a sponsor of the Artists Front to Win the War, cited by the House committee as a Communist organization.

The interrogation goes on in the written record for several more pages, with different members of the orchestra designated by number. One is said to have sold a car to the head of the Communist party, Earl Browder, with the implication of "guilty by association." Another had a wife who joined an organization targeted by HUAC and so on. McIlvaine was careful in his responses but stood his ground. This exchange took place toward the end of the hearing:

MR. SIKES. I assume that you are concerned about the allegations that have been made?

MR. McILVAINE. Yes; very much.

MR. SIKES. And if those allegations are correct then there would be good reason to believe that the work done by the members of this group against the interests of the United States and the democracies, done in behalf of the Communist party, could have more than offset the good that would have resulted from the results as far as music lovers are concerned?

MR. McILVAINE. I do not want you to think that I believe that we should have any Communists in this program. However, the evidence that we have from the report on the trip was all favorable as far as the impact of the orchestra, as an orchestra, and we have not received any report about any deleterious activity of any individual member.

McIlvaine was able to testify to the trip's political success when he quoted an article from the *Manila Chronicle*. He noted that this newspaper, by its own admission, was generally critical of everything American and was not known for praising the United States in any way. The Symphony of the Air tour was not only praised but also held up as a model for the future:

> Once in a long while, America contrives to muster enough of her native genius to present to the rest of the world the best that she can give. When this happens, the bitterest critics of America and the American way of life restrain themselves.... [W]e wouldn't care if the State Department bombarded us with invasions of other symphony orchestras and with exhibitions of other American artists ... this is the propaganda we would go out of our way to welcome.... Be it Europe or Asia and should the United States Government adopt this propaganda as seriously and on as large a scale as it has adopted the program of military aid, all the evils with which America has been identified might be forgotten.

As a result of the hearing, the Symphony of the Air received no further bookings from the State Department. However, the program itself was not harmed. The President's Emergency Fund was transformed into permanent legislation on 1 August 1956, when the Eighty-Fourth Congress voted to pass Public Law 860, the International Cultural Exchange and Trade Fair Participation Act.

ANTA, *the Dance Panel, and Martha Graham*

When Eisenhower's Emergency Fund was approved in August 1954, the State Department established an interagency committee to oversee decision-making. At the head was Deputy Assistant Secretary of State for Public Affairs Robinson McIlvaine. Julius Seebach represented the USIA. The committee also consisted of representatives from the Departments of Defense, Labor, Health, and Education and from other agencies as appropriate.

The State Department personnel realized that a committee of this nature was not equipped to choose artists or to handle the numerous details regarding contracts, performance spaces, programs, travel arrangements, and schedules that would require attention. A contract was therefore signed between the State Department and the American National Theater and Academy (ANTA), authorizing ANTA to serve as professional administrative agent. ANTA had been established in 1935 by Congress as a tax-exempt, self-supporting organization:

> The corporation shall be nonprofit and without capital stock. Its purposes shall embrace: The presentation of theatrical productions of the highest type; The stimulation of public interest in the drama as an art belonging to the theater and to literature and thereby to be enjoyed both on the stage and in the study; The advancement of interest in the drama throughout the United States of America by furthering in the production of the best plays.... The further development of the study of drama of the present and past in our universities, college schools, and elsewhere.

The incorporation charter for ANTA, enacted by the Seventy-Fourth Congress under Public Law 199, included an impressive list of wealthy and culturally influential figures, such as the conductor Leopold Stokowski and the financiers John Hay Whitney, Otto H. Kahn, A. Conger Goodyear, and Edward M.M. Warburg."[1]

Although the founders of the organization faithfully attended meetings, they could not agree on its goals. After the Second World War, two individuals deeply involved in theater approached ANTA with a plan for a strong, decentralized national theater. One was Robert Porterfield, a founder of Virginia's Barter Theatre. The other, Robert Breen, was the founder of the Oxford Players, a touring repertory company that he subsequently codirected with his wife, Wilva Davis; during the 1930s both had worked with Chicago's WPA Federal Theater Project. In 1946 ANTA's Board adopted the Breen-Porterfield Plan, and Breen became executive secretary of the organization. Without taking a salary, he worked with a small group of volunteers. His apartment above the Hudson Theatre on West Forty-Fourth Street in New York City became ANTA headquarters.

Breen remained with ANTA until 1951, and under his leadership the organization thrived. A National Theatre Service was established that served as a clearing-house for theater activities and resources, including job placement and counseling, guest artist lists, and sourcebooks of theaters. With ANTA support, regional theater groups in places such as Dallas, Minneapolis, and Detroit created high quality productions. The New York Experimental Theatre, under ANTA's guidance, produced twenty-five innovative works, including Bertolt Brecht's *Galileo*, starring Charles Laughton. In 1949, a cooperative effort between the New York Investment Company and ANTA board members Robert Dowling and Roger Stevens, resulted in ANTA's taking over the old Guild Theatre, that now became known as the ANTA Playhouse.

In 1946, at the first general meeting of the United Nations Educational, Scientific, and Cultural Organization (UNESCO), an international clearing-house for theater was established. The following year, the International Theatre Institute (ITI) was created under UNESCO auspices. ANTA became the United States Center of ITI and a member of the United States National Commission for UNESCO; it was thus well-positioned for involvement in international cultural exchange. In January 1949 ANTA put together an exhibition on American children's theater that was shown at the Children's Theater of Johannesburg.

In June ANTA made possible American participation in the Hamlet Festival at Elsinore, Denmark. Through the ITI, ANTA was invited to bring its production of the Shakespeare play, directed by Robert Breen and Nat Karson for the State Theatre of Virginia. The Department of State worked out an arrangement with the United States Air Force to provide planes to transport the cast and the staff for the production. ANTA was responsible for raising the money to produce the play overseas. The official program carried blessings from President Harry S. Truman and Milton Eisenhower, then Chairman of the U.S. National Commission for UNESCO. In the foreword to the program, an unsigned statement made it clear that the presence of America was important:

> Twelve years ago the people of Denmark made a signal contribution to world relations and the world's culture by instituting the Hamlet Festival at Elsinore.... This year will mark the greatest distance a national company of players has journeyed to historic Elsinore.... The presence of an American company presenting "Hamlet" in the courtyard of Kronberg Castle marks a heartening step in the world's progress toward a more complete international exchange of art and culture, and it is through such exchanges that lasting peace and understanding can be achieved.[2]

In April 1951 ANTA was appointed the State Department's official agent in organizing and administering the American attractions for the first Berlin Cultural Festival, and Robert C. Schnitzer was named General Manager. The terms of the contract between ANTA and the State Department (represented by the Division of Exchange of Persons) required that ANTA provide performances in return for a grant-in-aid of $156,500. Schnitzer was in charge of negotiating the artists' services and fees; he also dealt with technical arrangements, hotel accommodations, and public relations on the Berlin side. Once the Festival was underway, he supervised all American artistic activities in Berlin while remaining in contact with Washington. This framework was repeated for the 1952 Berlin Festival.

In 1950, 1951, and 1953 ANTA helped make contacts and arrangements for tours of Ballet Theatre in Europe and Latin America, where it performed under the name American National Ballet Theatre. The company did not represent the United States as part of any official program of international exchange. Although programs listed State Department support, no money was provided by the government. This was a source of considerable frustration for Robert Breen as head of ANTA and for Blevins Davis, president of the Ballet Theatre Foundation.[3]

With no help apparently forthcoming for the first tour, Davis wrote directly to President Harry Truman. His letter, written on ANTA stationery, secured limited embassy support for the 1950 European tour. For the company's 1951 Latin American tour, he was able to get the State Department to cable various embassies indicating their support but stopping short of a full commitment. "The Department has not committed the missions to any particular form of assistance in these matters, but has indicated that the missions will give all possible assistance consistent with their overall responsibilities and with local conditions." ANTA was essentially left on its own to struggle with income tax, currency exchange, and dollar transfer problems as well as coping with the vagaries of state-run theaters. A letter from Davis to Breen summed up the difficulties: "Incidentally all South American impresarios are under the impression that Ballet Theatre's tour is under the backing of the State Department and that the proposition is consequently a non-commercial one. To their greatest disappointment I have now to explain to them that we have the moral backing but not a financial one."[4]

It was only natural that the State Department would turn to ANTA when Eisenhower's Emergency Fund was set up. In 1954, Robert Dowling, a New York businessman and chairman of ANTA's Board of Directors, was appointed chair of the organization's International Exchange Program to handle the new government program and was authorized to form a committee from the Board to assist him. Robert C. Schnitzer became general manager in charge of daily operations, including direct contact with the State Department and ANTA's Board.

Conversations about ANTA's involvement began almost as soon as

Congress authorized the President's Emergency Fund, and a letter dated 20 September 1954 outlined a tentative agreement. Under its terms, a total of $75,000 was to be allocated to ANTA for salaries, office expenses, and travel.[5]

One of the most unusual and innovative aspects of the ANTA operation was the establishing of separate panels of experts in music, dance, and theater to choose the various presentations. This was Robert Dowling's idea and part of his original vision of how the program should work. He felt that only experts in each art form could make intelligent decisions about the best artists and groups that the United States should send abroad. None of the panelists received compensation, and each panel met once a month at the ANTA office. Initially, all the panelists were from New York, but soon there was a request to have representation from other parts of the country; the State Department agreed to underwrite travel costs.

The United States Information Agency (USIA) was another partner in the program. It was represented on the Operations Coordinating Board's Working Group for Cultural Activities and was also allocated $157,511 from the total five-million-dollar budget. It was the role of the USIA to publicize the program's artists and attractions, primarily through the embassies and, wherever possible, using the latter's cultural attachés. It was important to get advance press, radio, and newsreel coverage as well as reviews. Optimally, the USIA staff would help arrange lecture demonstrations, teaching stints, informal exchanges with local artists and community leaders, and formal receptions with heads of state and dignitaries.

Interest and expertise in the arts varied enormously among the embassy personnel assigned to these duties. There were those who neither knew nor cared about the arts; there were some who were initially cool to the program but were later won over; there were some who were passionate supporters from the start. In many countries American performances were a rarity. Issues arose concerning the suitability of theaters, and there were always unexpected financial and logistical problems.

Productions run into problems even when circumstances are normal and managers experienced. These were not normal circumstances. As indicated by the field reports, the difficulties were constant, if occasionally amusing. In Formosa in 1955 there was no concert piano for the Symphony of the Air; in several cases the promised military transport did not materialize. Costumes would disappear or get torn, music would get lost, artists would become ill, local officials were not told about a performance. In some cases local expenses were higher than anticipated; box office receipts could not be transferred into dollars or used to purchase local airline transportation.

When Schnitzer assumed the job of general manager, he realized that more information was needed to facilitate bookings in the Middle and Far East. In 1954 Edward Mangum and John Stark, two men with theater backgrounds, were asked to conduct professional surveys in these areas. The assignment, indicated Schnitzer in the Inter-Agency Committee Report he submitted on December 8, included "interviews with U.S. officials, local government officials, local theatre leaders and important local citizens, to determine the nature of the theatrical facilities available, the local booking techniques and offices, suitability for the public of all varieties of performing arts, the availability of financial or other assistance locally."

Who decided which attractions went where? All parties had a role in the decision-making process. The State Department, for instance, decided which countries and geographic areas were important to American foreign policy and would benefit from an American cultural presence. Often the USIA would be involved in the discussion; sometimes it would be influenced by requests from embassies for performances in general or for specific kinds of groups. Sometimes the panels would suggest a particular group as being most suitable for a specific country or area.

Artists or groups were sometimes suggested by State Department and USIA personnel. These suggestions might be based on first hand knowledge of an artist or group, the needs of a particular area, the likes or dislikes of a cultural attaché or a Washington administrator, or the desire of a member of Congress to promote hometown talent. For the most part, however, suggestions for artists came from the ANTA panels. As far as the records show, projects rejected by the panels at their monthly meetings were not sent abroad. There were instances when panel-approved projects were turned down by the Inter-Agency Committee; this might happen for a number of reasons, including budgetary considerations, geographic emphasis, or the needs of a particular area. Sometimes, performers might be shifted to the "Leaders and Specialists" category, a USIA exchange program administered by the State Department. This program sent individuals or small units abroad to teach.

Panel members consisted of critics, performers, choreographers, playwrights, composers, arts administrators, and ANTA representatives. The desired number of members on any given panel was fifteen; occasionally, State Department officials would attend panel meetings to discuss particular issues and answer questions. Not all panelists attended the monthly meetings on a regular basis, but they took their responsibilities very seriously. If they were not present at a meeting, they were informed about it and often responded by telephone or letter. There were open disagreements among panelists, and voting was used to resolve major issues. Some discussions extended over months.

Panel meetings were organized and administered by ANTA. Beverly Gerstein, a member of the ANTA staff who later worked in the USIA arts exchange program, was responsible for much of the coordination. Panels usually did not meet during the summer, and if emergencies arose great care was taken to solicit votes and opinions from everyone. Monthly reports from ANTA's Robert Schnitzer to the Inter-Agency Committee for the State Department covered panel discussions as well as reports and problems from the field.

In June 1955 the Music Panel consisted of J.S. Harrison, music critic, *The New York Herald Tribune*; Edwin Hughes, National Music Council; Carlton Sprague Smith, Chief, Music Division, New York Public Library; Virgil Thomson, composer and conductor; Olin Downes, music critic, *The New York Times*; Howard Hanson, composer and conductor; Paul Henry Lang, musicologist and music critic; William Schuman, composer, conductor, and president of the Juilliard School; Harold Spivacke, Chief, Music Division, Library of Congress; and Al Manuti, President of Local 802, American Federation of Musicians.

The Drama Panel members were Oscar J. Campbell, Professor Emeritus, Columbia University, and member of the Pulitzer Prize Committee; George Freedly, Curator of the New York Public Library Theater Collection, drama critic, *The Morning Telegraph*, and member of ANTA's Board of Directors; John Chapman, drama critic, *The Daily News*; Richard Coe, drama critic, *The Washington Post*; Rosamond Gilder, writer, drama critic, and director of the United States Center of the International Theatre Institute; Walter Kerr, drama critic, *The New York Herald Tribune*; Herman Levin, President of the League of New York Theaters; Alfred Lunt, actor; and Tom Prideaux, entertainment editor, *Life Magazine*.

Walter Terry and Emily Coleman at a party, 1950s. Photo by Roderick MacArthur. Dance Collection, The New York Public Library for the Performing Arts, Astor, Lenox, and Tilden Foundations.

The members of the Dance Panel were Lucia Chase, director of the Ballet Theatre Foundation; Emily Coleman, music and dance editor, *Newsweek*, and member of the Music Critics Circle of New York; Hyman Faine, Executive Secretary, American Guild of Musical Artists; Doris Humphrey, choreographer and member of the faculty of the Juilliard School; Lincoln Kirstein, general director of the New York City Ballet; Walter Terry, dance critic, *The New York Herald Tribune*; Martha Hill, director of the Dance Department, the Juilliard School; Bethsabée de Rothschild, head of the Rothschild Foundation, benefactress of ANTA, and patron of modern dance festivals held in 1953 and 1955 in New York.

At the end of 1955, choreographer Agnes de Mille joined the Dance Panel. In 1956 four critics were added to the Panel to provide wider geographic representation—Margaret Lloyd, who wrote for the Boston-based *Christian Science Monitor*; George Beiswanger, who wrote from Atlanta for

Former Dance Panel members Martha Hill (far left), Walter Terry (fourth from left), Agnes de Mille, and Lucia Chase at the Seventeenth Annual Capezio Dance Awards, 1968. The others are Ben Sommers (left), P.W. Manchester, John Hightower, and Arnold Sommers. Dance Collection, The New York Public Library for the Performing Arts, Astor, Lenox, and Tilden Foundations.

Theatre Arts, Dance News, Dance Observer, and *Dance Magazine;* Alfred Frankenstein, music and art editor of *The San Francisco Chronicle;* and John Rosenfield, theater editor and music critic of *The Dallas Morning News.*

John Martin, the dance critic of *The New York Times,* declined to join the Panel. An article published in *Dance News* in January 1955 explained why:

> Martin said that he was of the opinion that directors of dance organizations which are potential beneficiaries of the International Exchange Program should not be on the Panel, or if some persons heading dance attractions are invited to serve, all other persons heading dance attractions should also be invited. He added that his decision does in no way impinge the impeccable ethical standard of the persons involved or lessen his personal high opinions of them.[6]

When the Dance Panel met in January 1956, it discussed Martin's remarks. A summary of the discussion is given in the minutes for that meeting:

> It was felt that he refused because Lincoln Kirstein and Lucia Chase were on the Panel, and he did not think it fair for representatives of companies who would be participating in our program to be present. However, it has been agreed that these two Panel members will not vote on any companies that can be considered directly competitive to them.

Martin remained a problem for the Dance Panel. The minutes for the December 1955 meeting read: "Mr. Martin continues to think there is something 'phony' about the Program, and especially Mr. Kirstein's and

Miss Chase's membership on the Panel, since they have been helped by the Program." Presumably, there was some discussion of the issue, given what follows next in the minutes: "However, we feel that since we are going to use their companies anyway, as they are the best in the field, we should have the benefit of their advice and experience on the Panel."

The policy issue regarding conflict of interest was not finally resolved until the October 1956 meeting. At that time the Panel resolved that those "members having close professional ties with a specific organization and/or artist refrain from voting when a subject affecting their interests is proposed." In the final version the word "professional" was eliminated, and those with conflicting interests were enjoined from participating in the discussion as well as the voting. Since discussion carried a lot of weight and influenced the final vote, it was also agreed that "Panel members having close ties with a specific organization and/or artist [shall] refrain from voting or participating in discussion when a subject affecting their interest is proposed."

The links between foreign policy and cultural diplomacy and between State Department issues and Dance Panel deliberations are evident in the decision to send Martha Graham to Asia in 1955. The State Department made it clear to ANTA that Asia was an area of concern—one where political and military issues were paramount and cultural export could be valuable. The Dance Panel minutes of the January 13 meeting noted that Martha Graham "does not want to go to the Orient at this time, but wishes to return to Europe." The panelists took it upon themselves to persuade her otherwise: "Mr. Terry thinks that she could be talked into going to the Orient, and he will speak to her about this. Everyone would like to see her there. Miss Hill said she will also try to persuade her."

The specific area of concern for the United States in 1954, when these discussions began, was Southeast Asia. Eisenhower, prompted in large part by France's losing battle against nationalist forces in Vietnam, spelled out the domino theory in relationship to Southeast Asia at a news conference on 7 April 1954.[7] The idea was that if one nation in that area fell to Communism, the others would inevitably follow, thereby creating a politically dangerous situation. Asked to comment by a reporter on the strategic importance of Indochina to the free world, the President replied:

> You have, of course, both the specific and the general when you talk about such things. First of all, you have the specific value of a locality in its production of materials that the world needs. Then you have the possibility that many human beings pass under a dictatorship that is inimical to the free world. Finally, you have broader considerations that might follow what you would call the "falling domino" principle. You have a row of dominoes set up, you knock over the first one, and what will happen to the last one is the certainty that it will go over very quickly. So you could have a beginning of a disintegration that would have the most profound

influences.... Asia, after all, has already lost some 450 million of its peoples to the Communist dictatorship, and we simply can't afford greater losses. But when we come to the possible sequence of events, the loss of Indochina, of Burma, of Thailand, of the Peninsula, and Indonesia following, now you begin to talk about areas that not only multiply the disadvantages you would suffer through loss of materials, sources of materials, but now you are talking really about millions and millions and millions of people.[8]

The Geneva Conference met from 8 May to 21 July 1954 to deal with events in Indochina. Delegates came from the United States, the Soviet Union, the People's Republic of China, Great Britain, France, India, North and South Vietnam, Laos, and Cambodia. From the conference emerged a series of agreements, called the Geneva Accords, that called for a cease-fire in Vietnam and prohibited the introduction of new troops. The United States did not sign the accords, but pledged to respect them; the North Vietnamese delegation also refused to sign.

Less than six weeks later the Manila Pact was signed, and the Southeast Asia Treaty Organization (SEATO) was formed. SEATO was a regional organization of countries allied with the U.S. that provided for joint defense of the region against so-called Communist aggression.

In October 1954, the Vietminh, the Communist-led nationalist movement of Vietnam, defeated the French at Dien Bien Phu, spelling the end of French colonialism in the region. The French defeat raised concern in the United States among those who now feared either significant aggression by Communist China in the region, or an increase in Communist pressures on Southeast Asian countries. Secretary of State John Foster Dulles believed firmly in the desirability of containment policies based on regional military alliances, and the State Department was instructed to pay close attention to Southeast Asia.

According to historian Russell H. Fifield, "Washington accepted heavy security commitments in Southeast Asia in 1954."[9] The region had assumed significant military, economic, and political importance to the United States. "In broader dimensions the achievement of paramountcy by Communist China over Southeast Asia, it was believed in 1954, would give Peking a strategic position."[10] Countries such as India, Burma, and Indonesia, had only recently won their independence from colonial powers.[11] These countries, in addition to others in Southeast Asia, had strong Communist parties vying for control in new and often unstable governments.

Martha Graham went abroad and conquered; her company was seen by cheering thousands. The tour could have been problematic, for she was sent to areas where there was anti-American feeling and where her work was totally unknown. Her choreography was not easily accessible, and even in the United States she did not enjoy a mass following. But the foreign press and heads of state applauded. We had sent them an American art they respected, responded to, and had never dreamed existed. From 23 October 1955 to 12 February 1956, Graham and her company performed in Burma, India, Pakistan, Japan, the Philippines, Thailand, Indonesia, Malaya, and Ceylon.

Since the late 1920s, Martha Graham had stood at the forefront of the American modern dance movement. She had developed a strikingly original movement vocabulary and an equally original form of dance theater that integrated themes of myth, gender, and psychology with an avant-garde treatment of narrative. By the early 1950s her reputation was solidly established, and there was very little question about her contribution to the American arts.

One of Graham's landmark works was *Lamentation* (1930), a stark, powerful solo that was an abstract rendering of grief. *Primitive Mysteries* (1931) was another sparse, unsentimental dance, an ecstatic group work inspired by Hispano-Indian rituals honoring the Virgin Mary. In the late 1930s Graham acquired her first male partner, Erick Hawkins, and in *American Document* (1938) began to explore male-female relationships and sexual anxieties, key themes of her later choreography. She worked with a loose narrative structure and a spoken text, which included the Gettysburg Address, the Declaration of Independence, and Walt Whitman poems. *Every Soul is a Circus* (1939) marked Graham's further devel-

The Martha Graham Company in Japan, October 1955. Dance Collection, The New York Public Library for the Performing Arts, Astor, Lenox, and Tilden Foundations.

opment as a choreographer of theatrical forms that were dramas in movement. *Letter to the World* (1940), based on Emily Dickinson's poetry, explored the poet's real and imaginary world.

Graham took ten of her dances to the Far East. The most popular were *Appalachian Spring* (1944), *Cave of the Heart* (1946), *Night Journey* (1947), *Diversion of Angels* (1948), and *Seraphic Dialogue* (1955).[12]

Appalachian Spring had four archetypal American figures—Husbandman, Bride, Pioneer Woman, Revivalist. The work was about love's joys and fears, and about the emotional confrontation between new frontiers and established boundaries. The music by Aaron Copland was based on a traditional Shaker hymn; the set by Japanese-American sculptor Isamu Noguchi was abstract and symbolic. An Indian reviewer felt the dance was a "much-needed corrective to be set against the picture of the fat, well-fed, cigar-smoking American."[13]

Martha Graham in Lamentation, *1939. Photo by Barbara Morgan. Barbara Morgan Archives.*

The Asian audiences responded most powerfully to *Cave of the Heart* and *Night Journey*, modern retellings of ancient tragedies with sets by Noguchi. The first work, based on Euripides's *Medea* and with music by Samuel Barber, was a chilling story of tortured passion, in which the heroine killed her husband Jason and their children in revenge for his infidelity. The theme of *Night Journey* was the doomed fate of Jocasta and Oedipus; the work is charged with foreboding, especially the sequences involving the blind seer Tiresias and the chorus. The music by William Schuman underscored the erotic imagery and the inevitability of the final tragedy.

The other two dances that were favorites on tour were lighter in tone and more lyrical in movement. *Diversion of Angels* was a celebration of love, with couples performing duets that were playful, serious, and flirtatious. Graham had once again collaborated with Schumann and Noguchi, although the latter's set was soon discarded. *Seraphic Dialogue*, finished shortly before Graham left for the Far East, had Joan of Arc as its protagonist. Three dancers represented her life as a maiden, warrior, and martyr; the work ended on an ecstatic note, with Joan's symbolic ascent to heaven. Noguchi's set created a soft, shimmering environment, while the score by Norman Dello Joio underscored the themes of spiritual strength and hope.

In addition to performing, the company presented lecture-demonstrations on the Graham technique.[14] It also took part in various social and

Martha Graham as Jocasta in Night Journey.
Dance Collection, The New York Public Library for the Performing Arts, Astor, Lenox, and Tilden Foundations.

Martha Graham as Medea in Cave of the Heart. *Dance Collection, The New York Public Library for the Performing Arts, Astor, Lenox, and Tilden Foundations.*

diplomatic functions. The tour began in Japan on October 23. In Tokyo four performances were given in a 2,000-seat theater packed with standees. In 1956 *Dance Observer* published two short articles about the tour with excerpts from reviews of the company in Japan and elsewhere.[15] The English is often awkward, and the translations literal, but the enthusiasm is clear. A Japanese critic remarked: "Calmness to motion, motion to serenity…those two and a half hours gave whole audience deep emotion; even noticed lot of young dancers had swimming eyes with high praise." Another critic found Graham's discipline astonishing: "She started practicing the next day, which was never known for any foreign dance company to come over to Japan without allowing time to rest, showed her fighting spirit. We can see her full of energetic power in her slender body."

At least one reviewer felt that Graham's work revealed similarities with Kabuki: "Mystery, sensitivity, full of joy and sorrow that made some confusion still so well

designed into abstractive ideas. Some ways similar to Japanese Kabuki *Chiuta Mai* but greater space is controlled sharply."

The next stop was Manila, where the company gave three performances and one lecture-demonstration. The performances were the great social event of the season. *The Manila Evening News* wrote that Graham's choreography "celebrates the beauty and reality of the human body, even as it claws deep into the human heart." In Bangkok, there were six performances, and a lecture-demonstration that was attended by 3,000 students; in Singapore three performances and one lecture-demonstration were given. In Kuala Lumpur and Penang the company gave only lecture-demonstrations.

From Malaya the company went on to Indonesia, a country whose government was known to be critical of the United States. In Jakarta four performances were scheduled, and a lecture-demonstration that had to be moved to a larger hall to accommodate the crowd of more than 2,000 that materialized. The season sold out even before the company arrived; a student matinee sold out in twenty minutes. *Dance Observer* reported that "an editorial appeared in a Communist, anti-American newspaper so complimentary and enthusiastic that Washington officials have wirelessed it around the world."

Meeting and greeting: Martha Graham as diplomat during the 1955 Asian tour. Dance Collection, The New York Public Library for the Performing Arts, Astor, Lenox, and Tilden Foundations.

At the March 1956 hearing before the Committee on Foreign Affairs, Theodore Streibert, head of the USIA, read excerpts from Djakarta newspapers written during Graham's tour. He quotes one as saying: "Miss Graham has dispelled the prevalent notion that Americans live in a cultural wasteland peopled only with gadgets and frankfurters and atom bombs." Another paper commented more on the political impact. "If ever this paper came perilously close to forgetting its policy of leaning neither to the East or to the West, it was during Martha Graham week, because this talented woman presented something of the United States that we could wholeheartedly approve of."

Only rave reviews were heard in Rangoon, the company's next stop (December 13–18), the capital of a country known for the strength of its Communist movement and anti-Americanism. The February *Dance Observer* reported that well over 6,000 people attended the opening-night performance. It also published an excerpt from Prime Minister U Nu's statement in the *Burma Star*:

> Of one thing I am sure, Miss Martha Graham's performance will find enthusiastic audiences here as I understand that her theatre is very close to the classical Greek theatre which has many similar features to the Burmese theatre.... In one of my speeches at a public function in Moscow, in the course of my recent tour in the Soviet Union, I stressed the importance of personal contacts in international relations. I mentioned the names of outstanding Soviet artists who I consider would be excellent cultural ambassadors in other countries. In the same context I mentioned the names of outstanding American artistes, who, I believe, would serve the same purpose, and among them was Miss Martha Graham who is making her debut in Rangoon tonight.... Artistes like Miss Graham can very effectively contribute towards international goodwill and therefore they are a potent force for peace.

Dance Observer reported that after opening night the Burmese government bought 1,000 tickets for each remaining performance. The article quoted the *Burma Star*: "Many of us who went...to see a cheap exhibition of American limbs were disappointed. As a matter of fact, fools that came to scoff, stayed to pray."

The State Department was delighted with Graham's success in Japan, the Philippines, Thailand, Indonesia, Malaya, Burma, and Ceylon. They wanted her to continue on to India and Pakistan, countries with strong Communist parties and a long history of anti-American sentiment. The $200,000 allocated by the State Department for Graham's tour was insufficient for performances in India and Pakistan. As noted in the minutes of the December 1955 Panel meeting: "There was a slight overestimate of income, and underestimate of costs." Given the political importance of India and Pakistan, the State Department decided to allocate the additional amount. The company's first stop in India was Calcutta. The critic of the *Hindustani Standard* wrote: "Too often the United States came to us in the shape of cheap movies and magazines; in introducing us to this other face of her great country, Miss Graham is visibly raising Indo-U.S. relations to a higher level."

The 1955–1956 tour was enormously successful. Graham's message was universal and reached across many barriers. Asked by a leftist reporter, "Why are there no dances in your company in which the subject is universal brotherhood?" she responded: "There are no dances in my company in which that is not the subject. I could not do a single step if I did not believe in brotherhood. But I am not a propagandist. I don't need to make dances that say they are about brotherhood. All of my dances are."[16] Graham was an American artist whose voice spoke to the world in a language of inner experience.

A close look at the Panel minutes over the next few years shows that choices were not always easy and often occasioned lengthy discussion. Some of the issues were entertainment versus art; how best to represent the diversity of the American heritage; what role idioms other than modern dance and ballet (such as tap and jazz) should have in the program; the role of less established artists; how to deal with difficult work; was the target audience an educated elite or a mass public?

"What are we trying to say to the world at large?" asked panelist Hyman Faine at the December 1958 meeting. "Are we trying to present the best of American dance, music, and drama and hope their worth will create the audience, or are we going to make it sufficiently popular to assure an audience?"

Lincoln Kirstein, at the same meeting, made his views very clear: "A Martha Graham is remembered longer than a juggling act, and the residual effect of a serious project remains long after it leaves the area; the immediate effect of light entertainment is a short-range affair." Paine echoed Kirstein's sentiments: "The whole purpose of this program is to counteract the impression of life in America as shown in the motion pictures."

Many of the overseas embassies pressured the State Department to send popular entertainment. Discussing this issue at the December 1958 meeting, the Dance Panel agreed "that stimulating an audience is more lasting than simply diverting them, and it is important to show a side of our cultural life that is not known to other countries."

All members of the Dance Panel were comfortable with their early decisions to send the Limón and Graham companies abroad as cultural ambassadors. They knew the work of both artists intimately and regarded their innovations in technique and choreography as acceptable. Both, moreover, were perceived as upholding the standard of high art in dance while also appealing directly to audiences.

The Dance Panel was less comfortable with choreographers who had struck out in new directions and were considered avant-garde. As early as 1955, controversy had arisen among the panelists about Merce Cunningham and Alwin Nikolais. Both were experimenting with movement that was devoid of emotional and psychological content, but depended for its effect on an interplay of sight and sound, tension and texture.

In the 1930s Martha Graham had startled audiences by creating dances that externalized the protagonist's inner drama. In the 1950s Cunningham alienated many dancegoers by choreographing movement phrases where drama and meaning resided in the excitement of seeing changes of rhythm, space, shape, dynamics, and energy. The notion that avant-garde experiments of a new generation could be challenging to audiences here and abroad was difficult for the Dance Panel to accept.

The 1950s brought significant changes to concert dance in America. Members of the Dance Panel were in a quandary as they struggled with the new body of work emerging from the studios of the most talented and interesting of the young generation of choreographers. Because the panelists often found it difficult to accept this work, they frequently refused to sponsor it abroad. Many feared that sending these choreographers abroad as cultural representatives would elicit a negative response.

The issue arose early in the Panel's history. In February 1955, Merce Cunningham was presented to the Dance Panel as part of a package approved by the Music Panel for a tour with composers John Cage and David Tudor who would be playing their own work. The minutes indicate that the response of the Dance Panel was clearly negative:

Merce Cunningham at Jacob's Pillow, 1955. Photo by John Lindquist. Courtesy of the Harvard Theatre Collection, The Houghton Library.

> The Music Panel has approved the musicians, but the Dance Panel felt that it is too avant-garde and controversial. We would have to prepare the field for this type of entertainment. Perhaps after the first attractions go abroad this would be more suitable. The Music Panel felt it would be fine for the Orient, and Mr. Faine said that the people in the Orient would see and hear more in this music than would the Western World. Mr. Kirstein felt that the company was boring. The opinion of the Panel was that this could not be recommended for touring for at least a year.[1]

The following month, the Panel considered an appeal from John Cage. There is no indication that Cage appeared in person; most likely he voiced his complaint in a written rebuttal. The minutes recorded: "Mr. Cage does not want to go as a separate music project, but with the Merce Cunningham dance group." Kirstein felt the Cunningham group "would have considerable success in avant-garde groups in Germany, France, Italy and Japan." The Panel recommended that "we consider them to go only to Japan and India to play for intellectual groups where they have been requested. This discussion will be deferred to a future meeting."

At the next Panel meeting, Virgil Thomson came in person to present the majority views of the Music Panel. He reported that Cunningham had engagements in India, Ceylon, and Thailand, and the potential for dates in Indonesia. The company had also been invited by universities and dance groups "in an interchange of ideas on an educational and participational basis, something which many of the groups could not do. This would be 'intellectual and artistic fraternization.'"

Thomson told the Dance Panel that the Cage project would not "interfere with Martha Graham as it is not the same thing." He said that Cage knew what the project would cost "and could raise a good part of it himself if ANTA will accept it artistically." Lincoln Kirstein "felt that since they have so many bona fide invitations, he does not see what reason we can give for refusing our help. Aside from the way the Panel feels about Merce Cunningham's dancing, perhaps the Orient would like it."[2]

Panelist Martha Hill was very much against sending Cunningham abroad and voiced her opinion in no uncertain terms:

> Miss Hill felt that people who see Merce who have not seen Martha will have a strange idea about American dance. John Cage is more representative as a musician than Merce is as a dancer. He is "way out on the fringes of American dance," and is confusing and abstract. Three or four other companies would be more interesting and more representative.

The discussion at the October meeting about the Cage-Cunningham project had negative undertones throughout. Doris Humphrey feared that sending them would set a bad precedent—"that anyone who is energetic enough to go ahead and get bookings will get the okay from us. Many people would do this; however, it is not a good idea to send someone in whom we do not believe." She suggested that if a project involved two panels, representatives should get together for a review and then provide an answer.

Since the Music Panel had already approved the project, "it was suggested that the entire project be removed from the purview of the Dance Panel and presented as a music project, with Merce Cunningham as a disciple of Cage, an extension of his music." When it was made clear that Cunningham planned to take a company of seven rather than performing only as a soloist, Martha Hill wanted to know if Cunningham "would consider going without the company, because with many dancers it would have to be presented as a dance company." Although none of the other panelists are mentioned by name, the discussions continued about allowing the Music Panel to send John Cage, and perhaps allowing Cunningham to accompany him as a secondary part of the project. Finally, after much discussion, "it was decided that the Panel would ask John Cage to present a new plan for a recital demonstration on contemporary music, in association with Merce Cunningham, with an accent on music. Under these conditions the project would be acceptable to the Dance Panel."

At the November 1955 meeting, the Cage-Cunningham project was definitively laid to rest. "The Panel considers Harry Partch even more contemporary and avant-garde than Cage, and Sybil Shearer better than Merce Cunningham, if we want to send this type of performer."[3] Shearer herself came up for review two years later.

Merce Cunningham was born in Centralia, Washington, and began his dance training there at the age of twelve. In 1937, after graduating from high school, he enrolled at the Cornish School in Seattle, where he met John Cage, who was then on the school's faculty. He studied with Martha Graham in the summer of 1939, when the Bennington School of the Dance was in residence at Mills College. Graham invited him to join her company. He arrived in New York the following September, and almost immediately found himself dancing a principal role in *Every Soul is a Circus*. Cunningham danced with Graham until 1945 and created leading roles in many dances, including *El Penitente*, *Letter to the World*, and *Appalachian Spring*.

Cunningham's first choreographic efforts dated to 1942, when he and two other Graham dancers, Jean Erdman and Nina Fonaroff, presented a joint concert. Two years later, he gave his first solo concert with composer John Cage, who since the 1930s had been exploring new ways to organize and create sound. For this concert, both worked with a common time structure; music and movement came together at key structural points, but otherwise the two were independent.

In 1948 Cage and Cunningham made their first U.S. tour. They spent the summer at Black Mountain College, a small college near Asheville, North Carolina, that encouraged the exploration of new ideas. By 1951, when he choreographed *Sixteen Dances for Soloist and Company of Three*, his first dance to use chance procedures, Cunningham had established himself at the forefront of the dance avant-garde. "This dance," he later explained, "was a series of solos, duets, trios and quartets with an over-all rhythmic structure relating the small parts to the large in both the dance and the music. The form of the dances was not thematic (it never has been), but objects in space relating to time; in this situation the relationship being pointed out by the dance joining with the music at structural points."[4]

Cunningham went on to explain how chance operated in the work: "the individual sequences," he wrote, "and the length of time, and the directions in space of each were discovered by tossing coins. It was the first such experience for me and felt like 'chaos has come again' when I worked on it."[5] In 1952, in *Symphonie pour un homme seul*, Cunningham applied chance processes to everyday movements and social dance steps. The same year he collaborated with Cage on a theater event at Black Mountain College that was a prototype of the "Happenings" of the 1960s.

In 1953, Cunningham presented his recently formed company at the Theatre de Lys in New York. The following year, he received a Guggenheim Fellowship, and, with his company, made his first United States tour. Yet, within a year, a jury of peers was questioning the very foundation of his work, his use of chance, and his rejection of emotional, symbolic, and mythical content.

In 1960 Cunningham and Cage were invited to a festival in Berlin and requested help with transportation. The Music Panel supported the proposal, but once again there was resistance from the Dance Panel. At the April meeting Martha Hill indicated that she did "not want to jeopardize Limón's appearances in South America by taking money away from this tour to support Merce Cunningham's tour." She was not alone in looking at the project with an unfriendly eye. According to the minutes, the Panel as a whole "felt that this team no longer does what they set out to do years ago, and no longer believes in whatever art form they are trying to express. They are more interested in making newspaper copy now. Mr. Cunningham has integrity as a performer and is very good, but the Panel would prefer it if he would come up with a project without Mr. Cage. The Panel voted not to approve the project."

Cunningham and Cage, along with dancer Carolyn Brown and composers Earle Brown and David Tudor, went off to Europe anyway, enjoying considerable success in Venice, Berlin, Munich, Cologne, and Brussels. By 1961 small cracks had begun to appear in the Panel's uniformly negative view of his choreography. He had received an invitation to go to Tokyo in spring 1962 with a company of ten dancers, Cage, David Tudor, and two technical people. A Japanese newspaper had agreed to pay the group's operating costs in Japan. Cunningham needed to raise money for the transportation costs and indicated to the State Department that he would be willing to go elsewhere after Tokyo. At the June 1961 the Panel agreed that "he had been very successful in Berlin." When it was pointed out that funding Cunningham would mean not sending the Jerome Robbins company to the Far East, dance historian Lillian Moore, an invited guest at this meeting, "felt if there was a choice between the two, there would be no

Viola Farber (left) and Carolyn Brown in Merce Cunningham's Summerspace, 1958. *Photo by Richard Rutledge. Courtesy Merce Cunningham Dance Company.*

question that Jerome Robbins is preferable."

Other Panel members were more positive. Although many strongly objected to Cage's music, there was considerable support for Cunningham both as a dancer and choreographer. Walter Terry moved "that we recommend the Merce Cunningham Dance Company to our dance pool, with the understanding that this is an entire dance program, and the music used will only serve as accompaniment." Terry's motion was seconded, but William Bales and Agnes de Mille wanted to defer a final decision until they could see performances of his most recent work during the summer. The motion to approve Cunningham was tabled until the fall, with the following comment: "It was agreed that Mr. Cunningham's work would stir up a lot of controversy, but

Merce Cunningham (left), Steve Paxton, and Carolyn Brown in Aeon, *1961. Photo by Richard Rutledge. Dance Collection, The New York Public Library for the Performing Arts, Astor, Lenox, and Tilden Foundations.*

whether this would be good or bad was questioned. It was also agreed that Merce Cunningham himself is a magnificent dancer, but as a choreographer, and as a representative of American dance, there are still some questions."

A breakthrough came at the Panel meeting the following September, when "it was decided that Mr. Cunningham and his company would be suitable for festivals, educational institutions and capital cities in Europe, with special audiences, and he would be endorsed for such appearances only if and when such an attraction is needed." Walter Terry thought that Cunningham was remarkable in some of his creations, and "when he is good, he is brilliant.... However, the new work, 'Aeon', is too long, and was a frightening experience. Mr. Cunningham has many other excellent works in his repertory, and is a beautiful dancer, with a very sophisticated approach to dance. He could be told which works would be suitable and which would not." Terry's arguments did not convince Martha Hill. "Miss Hill believes he and his company could be most valuable in an area in which the State Department has no particular interest; it would not be for South America, Africa, or Asia. Merce Cunningham needs a sophisticated audience, such as Europe or Tokyo." Panelist Emily Coleman was willing to take the risk of sending him, and reminded the Panel that they could not anticipate his reception abroad.

Cunningham was not the only avant-garde choreographer the Panel rejected in the 1950s. Alwin Nikolais gave the premiere of his first major group works in 1953 at New York's Henry Street Settlement House. His work startled and alarmed many; others found it original and exciting. Nikolais created dances that celebrated the body as moving sculpture, and he accompanied the choreography with electronic tape loops of his own compositions. In his work he was interested in exploring shapes, often using costumes (especially ones made of stretch fabric), props, and slide projections to further his explorations of the spatial dimensions of the human body in solos and groups. His interest in pure motion clashed with what he called "the self-expression rampant in the late 40s":[6]

> My theory of motion allowed me to divorce myself from the bounds of literalism and realism and to judge my design choices simply upon the base of visual kinetics. I didn't have to light Nureyev—I could light motion.... It is not that I don't believe in hero identification, even Nureyev—but I wanted man to be able to identify with things other than himself. This is the day of ecological and environmental visions. We must give up our navel contemplations long enough to take our place in space.[7]

In 1948 Nikolais became the resident director of the Henry Street Playhouse on New York's Lower East Side. Initially, his classes were filled with neighborhood children, but word soon spread in the dance community that something different and exciting was taking place in the Henry Street Studio. In teaching, Nikolais emphasized an understanding of the concepts of energy and space, and often used improvisation for students to explore movement ideas.

His own dance mentor was Hanya Holm, a German born-dancer who had worked closely with Mary Wigman, one of the leading German expressionist dancers of the 1920s and 1930s. Holm came to the United States in 1931 to open the New York branch of the Wigman school; in 1936, in response to growing anti-Nazi feeling in the dance community, she dropped the Wigman name. Her classes emphasized a conceptual approach to dance training, and students experimented with spatial and dynamic concepts. After World War II, she became a successful Broadway choreographer with a number of "hits" to her credit, including *Kiss Me Kate* and *My Fair Lady*.

The fact that Nikolais had a theater at his disposal allowed him to experiment with lights, props, projections, and electronic music. He called his work "total theater":

> My total theater concept consciously started about 1950, although the seeds of it began much earlier I'm sure. First was expansion. I used masks and props—the masks, to have the dancer become something else; and props, to extend his physical size in space. (These latter were not instruments to be used as shovels or swords—but rather as extra bones and

Members of the Alwin Nikolais company in Tensile Involvement, *1953. Photo by David Berlin. Nikolais/Louis Foundation for Dance.*

flesh.) I began to see the potentials of this new creature and in 1952 produced a program called Masks, Props and Mobiles. I began to establish the philosophy of man being a fellow traveler within the total universal mechanism rather than the god from which all things flowed. The idea was both humiliating and grandizing. He lost his domination but instead became kinsman to the universe.[8]

Nikolais's total theater engendered criticism and controversy. By the late 1950s, he was drawing standing room audiences to the Lower East side, and works such as *Prism* (1956) and *Totem* (1959) were sowing wonder and delight—as well as numerous imitations.

Dance critic Margaret Lloyd was not able to attend the October 1958 meeting but sent a letter suggesting "Alwin Nikolais and Merce Cunningham as possible dancers who might tour for the program, even though they might be regarded as too avant-garde and mystifying. They both have excellent companies and their works pique the imagination and these artists present views of dance and its endless possibilities for development." Lloyd also felt it would be a good idea to send abroad "those artists who are adventuring on a cultural level beyond easy grasp. Good thing for any public to have to reach once in a while."

The response to Lloyd's suggestion was negative. Nikolais was quickly dismissed. "His use of the body is inhuman. He used it as a 'mobile,' completely motionless at times. As a single attraction it is not representative of dance in general; if his work could be compared with someone else's on a

Alwin Nikolais in rehearsal at the Henry Street Playhouse,
1950s. Photo by Gene Dauber. Nikolais/Louis Foundation for Dance.

joint program, this might be feasible." Martha Hill commented "that his programs are often too long." As for Cunningham, Walter Terry remarked that "Merce Cunningham has added more material that is 'less mysterious' than he has offered in the past. We might tell him should we consider sending him out that he could do only certain of his compositions. We should have to assist in selecting the program." Terry also wanted to make sure that Lloyd was sent a letter of response stating that both Cunningham and Nikolais were "eligible to re-apply with new programs and new works."

By 1961 the Dance Panel was ready to reconsider Nikolais. At its December meeting the members discussed his request for a State Department tour and for support of his company at the Spoleto Festival in Italy. Martha Hill said she "would consider [the group] interesting in Europe, not as representative of American dance, but because of Mr. Nikolais' approach—the use of staging, settings, and visual effects. As a dance company it would not be appropriate for the President's Program to tour because it is not representative enough; some of his works are stunning, most are too long."

Another panelist, George Beiswanger, "found the company rhythmically exciting, and felt it would cause a great deal of discussion and controversy; it would be attractive to sophisticated European audiences." More general discussion was summarized in the minutes: "It was generally agreed that the stage effects and lighting are of genuine interest . . . but it was pointed out that 'a little goes a long way.'" The Panel came to the following conclusion: "For a Festival series in such a cultural center as Spoleto, the Alwin Nikolais New Theater of Motion (in a selected and shortened repertoire of his best works . . .) would be of interest to audiences, and would reflect one aspect of our dance theater well."

A new panelist brought fresh eyes to Nikolais's work. William Bales joined the Panel in 1961. A dancer and choreographer who had started out in the 1930s, he had concentrated since the early 1950s on teaching. At the February 1962 meeting he mentioned that he was "surprised and pleased" at a recent Nikolais performance." He still felt it was "particularly appropriate for a Festival audience; you can see it once and once only." But he liked it: "The impression is immediate, bizarre, fresh, experimental. It is true festival material, and more interesting than Merce Cunningham, although the latter is a much better dancer."

Several other artists considered by the Panel also diverged from the mainstream styles of 1950s modern dance. One was Sybil Shearer, whose name had come up in discussions about Merce Cunningham. In 1957 she approached the Panel about going abroad. The minutes of the September meeting recorded the members' response: "Although she is a marvelous dancer, as a performer she is unpredictable, and audiences often do not understand what she is doing. We should thank her for her interest, but at the present time she does not fit into the plans of our Program."

Although not widely known today, Shearer was considered one of the most interesting choreographers of the 1950s. She had been a member of the Humphrey-Weidman dance company in the 1930s and an assistant to Agnes de Mille in the early 1940s, working with her on the ballets *Three Virgins and a Devil* and *Drums Sound in Hackensack*. A concert of her own work in 1942 was singled out by the critic John Martin as the most promising choreographic debut of the previous year. In *Dance to the Piper*, de Mille recalled her impressions of Shearer's work:

> She announced an initial concert at Carnegie Chamber Hall. I asked to see her dances beforehand, with some sort of idea of editing.... The first two numbers were weak, I noted with no surprise, but then she suddenly let loose to something of Chopin, and all the pomposity and condescension left me.... I knew she was a technician, but she was dancing as few in the world can. She was composing as few seldom do including, most certainly, me. It became suddenly clear that Sybil had enormous gifts.... After her first New York concert six months later every dancer in the city knew she was a name to conjure with.[9]

Shearer moved to Chicago in 1942, although she continued to make annual New York appearances. By 1951, in *Once Upon A Time*, she had created a series of solos that formed an abstract cycle of dance. *Shades Before Mars* (1953) confirmed to those who saw her at the Brooklyn Academy of Music that she had a unique voice of her own. Over the years, her behavior became more and more erratic. Concerts would be scheduled, then suddenly and without explanation canceled. Few would have questioned the Panel's description of her as "unpredictable."

Another artist who was seriously considered by the Panel for support was Anna Sokolow. She had danced in the Graham company from 1930 to 1937 and was an important teacher and choreographer in her own right. She had worked abroad for long periods, first in Mexico, where she formed a company in the 1940s, and then beginning in the 1950s, in Israel. Unlike Graham and the other modern dance artists considered for support, she no longer danced.

Sokolow's most celebrated work was *Rooms* (1955), a powerful statement about the loneliness and despair of big city life, set to an original jazz score by Kenyon Hopkins. The dance opened with a group of people sitting in chairs, isolated from one another and from the world. In the sections that followed—"Dream," "Escape," "Desire," "Panic," the dancers gave searing portraits of people trapped in their bleak states of existence. *Metamorphosis* (1957) was based on Franz Kafka's short story about a man who woke up one morning and found he had become a bug. In the dance the audience discovers his hopeless, skewed reality.

Sokolow came up for discussion in March 1958 but did not pass muster. "Her work is good and very exciting," opined Walter Terry, "but certain of her chief works (*Metamorphosis* and *Rooms*) would escape foreign audiences. They are stimulating to Americans but they are confusing and depressing to an audience who have nothing to compare them with." This was an odd statement, as Sokolow had successfully created works in both Mexico and Israel. The Panel's final comment on Sokolow in 1958 echoed Terry's sentiments: "We should tell her that her application was considered along with the others, and while they have the highest respect for her as an artist, the Panel did not feel her repertory was suitable."

The Panel discussed John Butler on many occasions. However, despite considerable initial interest in his choreography, the members felt it was not original or important enough to send abroad. Finally, in 1961, he was recommended for touring support.

A native of Tennessee, Butler was a member of the Martha Graham company from 1945 to 1955. During this decade, he danced in *Oklahoma!* and did a fair amount of television work; he also created the dances for Gian-Carlo Menotti's *The Consul* (1947). In 1955, his John Butler Dance Theatre premiered *Clowns* and *Angels* at a festival in Italy. Two years later, he created *Seven Faces of Love* for American Ballet Theatre and staged Menotti's *The Unicorn, the Gorgon and the Manticore* at the Library of Congress.

A 1955 report of the Panel's reaction to an audition of the Butler company prompted an extensive discussion. "Miss Hill felt this was not the most representative group in America, and therefore should not go to areas that have not seen first-rate groups like José Limón or Martha Graham first." She is also quoted in the minutes as saying that she "would be ashamed of us sponsoring John Butler." Walter Terry was more positive: "The Butler group is a good company, with a musically interesting background, and very respectable." Emily Coleman wanted to support the Butler company "to go anywhere, as they had a fresh, young quality and a lot of talent." Lincoln Kirstein was also positive: "Although he is not an original artist, he is a good craftsman."

Doris Humphrey had reservations about some of Butler's work. This led to the following conclusion: "The Panel is all interested in his work, but they are not ready to give him carte blanche. Miss Humphrey wanted to know if we have the right to change or advise on programs of the artists overseas." Programming remained an issue with Butler when he became dance director of the summer Festival of Two Worlds, which Menotti had founded in Spoleto, Italy, in 1958. The Panel approved a request for assistance to transport twelve American dancers to Italy for the 1958 festival and provide living expenses for them during the rehearsal period. The dancers would be chosen by Butler and Jerome Robbins, both of whom would present their work on festival programs. Support for the dance portion of the Spoleto Festival was forthcoming again in 1959.

Until the early 1960s, John Butler had his own company; later, he chiefly worked with opera and ballet companies. He was one of the first to break the rigid barrier separating modern dance and ballet. Although his training and performance experience had chiefly been with Martha Graham, he was a popular choreographer for ballet companies. Two of his better-known works, *Carmina Burana* (1959) and *Portrait of Billie* (1961), displayed the musicality, solid craftsmanship, and powerful sense of movement for which he was best known. At the January 1961 meeting the Panel approved Butler's company as a potential dance export.

Erick Hawkins was another former member of the Graham company who applied to the Dance Panel for touring support. Trained chiefly in ballet, Hawkins joined the company in 1938, the first male dancer to become a member of what was until then an all-female group. He and Graham became lovers, and she created many important roles for him. In 1948 the two were married; in 1950 they separated, and he subsequently left the company.

Hawkins struck out on his own. In 1952, he collaborated with composer Lucia Dlugoszewski on *openings of the (eye)*, and five years later, created *Here and Now with Watchers*, a seventy-five-minute duet for himself and dancer Nancy Lang. This, too, was a collaboration with Dlugoszewski, who played her music on what she called a timbre piano, plucking the strings with wood, metal, and glass to create unconventional sounds. An important work for Hawkins, the choreography emphasized the immediacy of pure movement that was soft as well as mysterious. Hawkins said that he wanted to "show the identity of man and woman, not their struggle for domination, nor their aggressiveness toward each other."[10]

By 1960, when he choreographed *8 Clear Places*, Hawkins left his Graham heritage behind. His technique emphasized the free flow of movement while his choreography celebrated the mystical poetry of the soul and man's magical relationship to nature. The sections of the dance had titles such as "North Star," "Pine Tree," and "inner feet of the summer fly"; the music by Dlugoszewski was played live on instruments of her own invention made from glass, wood, metal, skin, and paper.

The minutes of the January 1961 meeting indicate that Hawkins wanted to tour with two or three dancers. He was interested in going to India, "whose minister of culture seems to want him." Hyman Faine said Hawkins was "a very good dancer, but we would have to see the program he has in mind." Hawkins approached the Panel again in 1962, this time requesting support for a tour of India and the Far East. The response was quite positive. "Miss Hill believes that this would be an extremely appropriate and effective program for those areas. He would be able to travel with only four people. One musician plays everything in his repertory; it would be very inexpensive and very special. The Indians have an empathy with the movement of his dances." William Bales urged the Panel to approve Hawkins for special assignments. "Erick Hawkins is the type of artist whom the Asia Society brings into this country; not a commercial artist, but an outstanding, unique, cultured person, and his works are worth sending to the Orient."

Jean Erdman joined the Graham company in 1938, the same year as Hawkins. She left it in 1943, to pursue her own choreography, although she returned as a guest artist in 1945 and 1946. During the 1940s she created many solos, collaborated with Merce Cunningham and Erick Hawkins, and also formed her own group, although she did not keep it together on a consistent basis. In 1945 critic Edwin Denby commented that Erdman's dances "suggested an anthropological fantasy and they had the tones of legendary games...she fascinated and delighted me. Whatever the piece was meant to mean, there was a lightness in the rhythm, a quality of generosity and spaciousness in the movement."[11] In a 1949 review of the group work *The Perilous Chapel*, Walter Terry commented that the dance was concerned with "spatial patterns, [and] designs in flux" and that it was "curiously restful (without being dull)."[12] When the Panel discussed Erdman at the May 1955 meeting, they decided she was "respectable, but not outstanding."

Paul Taylor was another applicant who had performed with Graham. A member of her company in the 1950s, he also danced with Merce Cunningham. Taylor began presenting his own work in 1955, and in time built up an eclectic, wide-ranging repertory with great popular appeal. *Three Epitaphs* (1956), *Epic* (1957), *Insects and Heroes* (1961), and *Aureole* (1962) were among the most important of his early works; all but one remain in repertory. Critic Edwin Denby wrote in 1964: "Taylor's choreography at his first recital...was antidance and avant-garde....He admired more than anything the shoreless beauty of Cunningham's dancing antidance, and he still does. But the more he danced and choreographed, the more a powerful and complexly fluid dance momentum engaged him."[13]

The Panel decided in September 1961 that "Paul Taylor is avant-garde, but not so much as Merce Cunningham. He is a marvelous performer, and his staging is more colorful than Cunningham's." The Panel members loved his onstage persona, but were cautious about his progress. They thought him "one of the most fabulous male dancers, but not seasoned yet." William Bales "felt he should be watched and encouraged, without making him any promises." This caution seemed to be generally agreed upon.

The panelists were not ready to endorse Taylor at their December meeting. "It was agreed that Mr. Taylor is a superb dancer, but as a choreographer, he has not yet arrived. He is one of the best male dancers in the country, and some day will perhaps succeed in creating fine dances too." The following September, however, they voted to endorse him. Lillian

Moore, who had recently joined the Panel, reported that the Taylor company "gave a very fine performance in Connecticut this summer and received rave reviews." She felt that it was "a beautiful little company, very finished, polished and theatrical. Although a bit 'out,' they are not 'far out' like Merce Cunningham, for example. They would have a wider appeal than Erick Hawkins, more romantic, theatrical, moving."

By 1962 the Dance Panel was definitely more receptive to choreographers outside the mainstream. Both the changing times and the addition of new members helped alter the perspectives of the Panel; what had seemed radical only five years earlier now began to seem acceptable. At the June 1962 meeting, there was discussion about artist Ann (now known as Anna) Halprin[14] and her group, The San Francisco Dancers' Workshop. Halprin's was the only American dance group invited to appear at the Venice Festival of Contemporary Music for 1963. Her collaboration with the Italian composer Luciano Berio was supposed to

Paul Taylor in Episodes, *1960. Photo by Carl Van Vechten. Courtesy of Joseph Solomon, as Executor of the Estate of Carl Van Vechten.*

be a high point of the Festival, and she was requesting support for some of her dancers and personnel. As recorded in the minutes, Halprin, according to her manager, "has arrived at a startling new form which has created an enormous amount of excitement."

Ann Halprin founded The San Francisco Dancers' Workshop in 1955 with a group of multidisciplinary artists; in 1959 they incorporated as a nonprofit organization to promote innovative work. Halprin wanted to explore connections between and among the arts and open up new possibilities for dance; she felt the traditional modern dance techniques had little to offer her. Her summer workshops, conducted outdoors on the dance deck attached to her house in Marin County, attracted a growing number of young artists in search of new possibilities.

In 1962 Halprin created *Five-Legged Stool.* In this full-evening work she rejected the proscenium stage and utilized all existing spaces; she made task movement rather than "dance" movement the basis of her choreography. She also explored using time units rather than movement phrases to create rhythm. Halprin utilized sound, voice, and movement to create her vision of total theater. Halprin wrote about the piece:

> There was an attempt to really break down cause and effect. I wanted everything to have such a sensory impact that an audience would not question why. I didn't want anything to look as if it had meaning, or con-

tinuity....It was a big thing for us—the first time we hadn't used tights and leotards....This was a very important breakthrough for us, and it helped us have completely new images of how we were....What happened was that the audience was in the center, and the performance went all around them.[15]

At the June 1962 meeting great interest was expressed in Halprin's work, and panelist Alfred Frankenstein, who wrote for *The San Francisco Chronicle*, was asked to submit reviews. When the Panel met the following September, it was reported that Frankenstein's reviews were extremely favorable; he had made a strong plea "to back the company to the hilt." Hyman Faine went to see the company when he was in San Francisco, and watched rehearsals for *Exposizione*, Halprin's collaboration with Luciano Berio. Faine reported back at the October meeting: "This work in progress is an excellent one....Although difficult to stage, it is very exciting and effective. This is a very small, select group, all of whom are actors as well as dancers. They do communal choreography, each working in relation to the other, improvising and changing the dance each time. It is very successful." Ultimately, however, the Panel decided not to support *Exposizione*, as it was an unknown quantity. It was felt Halprin should seek funding from private sources, as the Panel could not support her on the basis of only one work, *The Five-Legged Stool*. Most striking about the Panel's response to Halprin was its ready acceptance of her radical experiments.

By 1962, radical change was in the air. The first concert of the Judson Dance Theater took place in New York on July 6. Judson soon became a meeting ground for dancers, choreographers, composers, writers, and visual artists who had been exploring new ways of organizing movement and dance in a class taught by Robert Dunn at the Cunningham studio. A composer, dance accompanist, and student of John Cage, Dunn

Members of the Anna Halprin company in Exposizione, *1962. Courtesy of Anna Halprin.*

Doris Humphrey conducting a workshop at the Ninety-Second Street Y, 1950s.
Private collection, New York.

encouraged his students to experiment with time structures, chance meth-
ods, and anything else they could think of. Yvonne Rainer, Trisha Brown,
and Simone Forti had all met at Halprin's 1960 summer workshop. They
met up again in New York. By 1962 all three had worked with Robert
Dunn and became part of Judson Dance Theatre.

Most members of the Dance Panel were unwilling to support the
avant-garde choreographers of the 1950s and early 1960s. However, they
were interested in supporting young dance artists of high merit whose
work fell within more traditional boundaries. Panelist Doris Humphrey
captured the imagination of the other panelists when she suggested organizing a choreographic contest for small companies with tour support as a
prize.

The minutes of the April 1957 meeting indicate she presented her plan
with William Kolodney, Educational Director of the Ninety-Second
Street Young Men's and Young Women's Hebrew Association (YM-
YWHA), a major performance center for modern dance, where throughout the 1950s Humphrey had conducted a choreographic workshop.

The competition would be judged by an award committee of distinguished laymen and specialists. Those who wanted to compete would be
presented in performance at the YM-YWHA during the 1957–1958 season:

Each group's presentation would be limited to one-half hour. The company selected should have enough repertory to make up one or more complete programs. A variety of styles would be aimed for with a contrasting soloist. A professional director would be engaged under the sponsorship of the YM-YWHA Dance Center. Such a person could handle the innumerable details arising from the overwhelming number of participants expected. This kind of dance contest, already frequent in Europe, is a "first," badly needed to bring dance more in line with the other arts in America. The contest could not only bring to light unknown American dance work, but could also be of incalculable encouragement to the recipient and other young dancers, and the Brussels engagement would help the recognition of dance in our own country. The plan estimated a company of 20 or less, including manager and technicians, at a maximum cost of $35,000, for transportation and one week in Brussels.

The plan was accepted by the Panel but never carried out for several reasons. The funds for the 1958 Brussels World Fair had been slashed by Congress, and there was a good chance that the performing arts component would be eliminated or significantly reduced. The State Department felt that without the World's Fair appearance, since Limón was already touring Europe in 1957, an additional modern dance company would destroy the balance they sought.

The Panel recommended that Humphrey's idea be reconsidered for fiscal year 1959 either for Europe, including the Middle East, or for South America. The project was brought up again in other Panel meetings in 1957 but never came to fruition. Humphrey was absent from meetings during 1958 and passed away late that year; her innovative idea of a contest to bring forward younger, unknown talent was not brought up again.

Today, at Dulles or Kennedy Airport, travelers pay little heed to Aeroflot planes sitting majestically on the airstrip waiting to load passengers. Both American and Russian tourists, academics, artists, scientists, or businessmen can now take advantage of the Russian airline's new luxury service and fly back and forth to Moscow with relative ease. In addition, both Russians and Americans are becoming accustomed to visiting and working in each other's countries.

For those growing up today it would be hard—if not impossible—to imagine how miraculous this would have seemed at the height of the Cold War in the 1950s. Travel between the Soviet Union and the United States was almost unheard of, except under special agreements or for diplomatic reasons. The two countries were truly divided by the symbolic Iron Curtain; propaganda on both sides led to distrust, misinformation, hatred, fear, and paranoia. Russians with relatives in the United States were afraid to write letters or to communicate with them in any way, and the same held true for Americans with families in the Soviet Union.

It is in this context that the first exchange agreement between the two countries has to be understood. Signed on 27 January 1958, it was named the Lacy-Zarubin agreement for the two chief negotiators and signatories—William S. B. Lacy, President Eisenhower's Special Assistant on East-West Exchanges, and Gregory Z. Zarubin, Soviet Ambassador to the United States. The full title was "Agreement between the United States of America and the Union of Soviet Socialist Republics on Exchanges in the Cultural, Technical, and Educational Fields." Because it was an executive agreement rather than a treaty, it did not require Senate ratification.

As early as 1955 there had been an attempt on the part of France, America, and Great Britain to develop exchange programs with the Soviet Union. In that year, at the Geneva Foreign Ministers Conference, a proposal was made to the Soviet Union for a seventeen-point program to remove barriers to normal exchange in culture, education, books and publications, science, sports, tourism, and the information media. Foreign Minister Molotov rejected the proposal and accused the West of meddling in Soviet internal affairs. A change in policy occurred when Nikita Khrushchev attacked Stalin at the Twentieth Party Congress in February 1956. The result was a move toward peaceful coexistence and increased contact with the West, and almost immediately cultural agreements were signed with Belgium, Norway (1956), and France (1957).

Shortly after the 1955 Geneva Foreign Ministers Conference, some breakthroughs were made in Soviet-American artistic exchange. Carlton Smith, director of the American National Arts Foundation, traveled to Moscow. His negotiations with Nikolai Mikhailov, the Soviet Minister of Culture, led to several successful exchange visits of performing artists.

While *Porgy and Bess* was touring Europe in 1955, the company received an invitation from the Soviet Minister of Culture. For a period of almost three weeks, *Porgy and Bess* was a star attraction in the Soviet Union. These performances took place at the Palace of Culture in what was then Leningrad from 26 December 1955 through 5 January 1956, and then at Moscow's Stanislavsky Theater from January 10 to 17.[1] The previous October 3 the Soviet pianist Emil Gilels had arrived in the United States for a one-month tour, performing in New York, Chicago, Cleveland, Boston, and Washington. Six weeks later, on November 20, the Soviet violinist David Oistrakh made his American debut at New York's Carnegie Hall and also played in other American cities including Chicago, Washington, and Boston. Both artists came as a result of Carlton Smith's negotiations in Moscow.

In 1956 the Boston Symphony Orchestra received support from Eisenhower's International Exchange Program for a tour of Europe and the Soviet Union. As part of that tour, the orchestra, under the leadership of Charles Munch and Pierre Monteux, performed in Leningrad on September 6–7 of that year; this was followed by two days of concerts in Moscow.[2] During the spring of 1956, the American impresario Sol Hurok arranged tours of the Soviet Union for two of his most famous artists— the violinist Isaac Stern and the singer Jan Peerce. That same spring, Columbia Artists Management presented the Soviet cellist Mstislav Rostropovich on his first American tour.[3]

It looked as if there would be a large breakthrough when plans were announced by Hurok to bring the Moiseyev Dance Company to the United States in 1956. This was a company founded and directed by Igor Moiseyev with a repertory of highly theatricalized versions of folk dances from the many regions of the Soviet Union. A *New York Times* bulletin from Moscow, dated 16 March 1956, noted: "The ninety-member troupe...was warmly received last year in London, Paris, and other Western capitals....Letters providing for the engagement will be signed here tomorrow by Soviet officials and Sol Hurok."

Negotiations ultimately broke down because the Immigration and Nationality Act of 1952 (McCarran-Walter) required fingerprinting for foreign visitors. This impasse was the subject of a *New York Times* story published on June 1: "Nikita S. Khrushchev declared today that no Soviet citizen ever will submit to fingerprinting in order to visit the United States....He added that at the Geneva conference last year he had raised the issue with President Eisenhower. He said the result was that small groups of Soviet citizens could visit the United States on official passports without fingerprinting."[4] The official American stance was that official visas without fingerprints could not be issued to large groups such as the Moiseyev, and their fall tour never took place.

The 1958 US-USSR exchange agreement made it possible for the Moiseyev Dance Company to come to America. Under this two-year agreement there were exchanges in science, technology, agriculture, medicine, public health, radio and television, motion pictures, exhibitions, publications, government, youth, athletics, scholarly research, culture, and tourism. Also included was an arrangement to establish direct air service between the two countries.

The Moiseyev Dance Company took America by storm. With a company of 106, it was the first large Russian group to perform in America. The visit was the result of extensive efforts and negotiations on the part of impresario Sol Hurok.[5] In its eleven-week tour the Moiseyev performed in many cities, including New York, Philadelphia, Chicago, Los Angeles, and San Francisco. Newspapers reported that the group was seen by 450,000 persons and had grossed more than $1,600,000. Two weeks after performances began at the Metropolitan Opera House on April 14, a *New York Times* article carried this headline: "Scalpers Find 'Hottest' Tickets in Town Are for Russian Dancers at the 'Met.'"[6] The article went on to report that tickets marked at $8.05 were being sold for $80.00; one woman who had paid $3.00 for two seats but was unhappy with the view was able to sell her tickets for $10.00 within a few minutes.

An editorial in *Dance Magazine* in June 1958 commented on both the non-dance and dance aspects of the company's impact. "[The] dancers are magnificent.... Their subject material, stylized, still retains its warm-

The Moiseyev Dance Company in a Moldavian dance. Photo by Roger Wood. Dance Collection, The New York Public Library for the Performing Arts, Astor, Lenox, and Tilden Foundations.

hearted folk quality.... And there is the strong non-dance element—the indisputable excitement that comes of seeing Russians—real people—laughing, dancing, waving. For forty years the doors have been shut. We have known Soviet citizens only by hearsay."[7]

Newspapers all over the United States published numerous articles about the Soviet dancers, stories that brimmed with excitement and wonder at finally seeing people from that mysterious, closed-off country and at seeing the quality of their theatrical offering.[8]

The dance critic John Martin, who had not been a fan of international artistic exchange when the Eisenhower program began in 1954, was ecstatic. Martin's review in *The New York Times* on April 15 registered his excitement about the Moiseyev's opening night performance at New York's Metropolitan Opera House. "The implications of the occasion were enormous with regard not only to international relations but also to artistic exchange.... Under such circumstances, there might easily be a tendency to overrate the performance itself and regret it the next day. To play safe, then, let us risk understatement and call it merely stupendous." On the West Coast, *The Los Angeles Times* reported on May 18, "there was hardly a seat left for any performance. The Moiseyevs have already captured New York. According to all reports, the metropolis has not witnessed so much excitement in many a day."[9] The headline for a story in *The Philadelphia Bulletin* (June 13) read: "Moiseyev Dancers Win Ovation Here." The article noted that the advance publicity was accurate, and the company was indeed spectacular. "The huge auditorium was a wondrous spectacle of seething humanity as cries and applause greeted the Soviet dancers' impressive feats."[10]

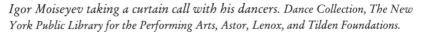

Igor Moiseyev taking a curtain call with his dancers. Dance Collection, The New York Public Library for the Performing Arts, Astor, Lenox, and Tilden Foundations.

Not content to report on their dancing, the press was delighted to tell readers about Soviet explorations of American life. On April 23, *The New York Times* carried a long story about a trip by some of the dancers to a beauty salon. "Four Russian women got a chance to explore an American woman's inner sanctum and they learned some of our beauty secrets."[11] According to the article, their biggest discovery was that beer helped in setting fine hair, a piece of information given to them by Kenneth, the star hairdresser of the Lily Daché salon, in exchange for a homemade henna recipe. "Russian women make their own henna," explained one of the dancers, "with egg, cocoa and salt. It is called the 'people's medicine.'"

Another Moiseyev excursion that brought attention in the press was a visit that sixty of them made to New York's Folk Dance House, run by Michael and Mary Ann Herman on West Sixteenth Street. The article in *The New York Times* was accompanied by a picture of Soviet dancers watching a demonstration of American folk dances.[12] They stayed for two hours, dancing "The Texas Scottische," "The Virginia Reel," and "The Sicilian Circle." When they danced a New Hampshire square dance with caller Ralph Page, "the Russians kept pace and sometimes set it." They also watched demonstrations of other dances, such as "Paw Paw Patch" and "Kentucky Mountain Running Set." The reporter observed: "Some of them, including Igor Moiseyev, the director, took notes prodigiously."

Perhaps most symbolic of mass interest and curiosity about the group was the fact that Ed Sullivan, host of the popular CBS variety show, invited them to perform for millions of Sunday-night viewers. According to Jack Gould, *The New York Times* television critic, Sullivan "devoted his full hour to the Moiseyev company, in itself a sensible and constructive innovation for Sunday-night variety on television."[13] The entire evening "scored a resounding hit.... Their fantastic agility, vigor and precision were almost unbelievable; their sense of excitement altogether contagious." On July 6 Gould wrote a follow-up article—based on the ratings in which he challenged the notion that a mass audience will not respond to quality entertainment. "According to the most revered video standards—the ratings—the Russian dancers outdrew both a top Western, 'Maverick,' and Steve Allen's variety show." Gould was aware that interpreting ratings could be tricky and never totally accurate. "But," he noted, "there's no question that millions did tune in the Russian folk dancing and stayed with it right to the end."[14]

The Moiseyev Dance Company consisted of highly trained dancers schooled in ballet and folk dance. The director, Igor Moiseyev, was a brilliant choreographer and artist who trained his dancers as virtuosos. The 1958 tour included the following numbers: *Suite of Old Russian Dances, Dance of the Tatars of Kazan, Yoruchka (A Byelorussian Dance), Khorumi (An Adzharian Dance), Polyanka (The Meadow), Zhok (A Moldavian Suite), Mongolian Figurine, City Quadrille, Bul'ba (Potatoes), Partisans, Soccer, Two Boys in a Fight,* and *Ukrainian Suite.* The public was treated to sophisticated, exuberant adaptations of folk material as well as contemporary choreography on Russian themes. One of the most memorable items was *Partisans*, a work that, according to the program, showed "the struggle against the Nazis in the region of the Northern Caucasus." Black-caped figures created compelling images as they moved swiftly across the stage in shifting patterns; these represented members of the Russian underground as they discovered a ravaged village.

When the Moiseyev Dance Company performed at Convention Hall in Philadelphia, a note was included in the program: "Knowing that basically there exists no ill will between the people of the United States and those of Russia, we want to say 'It is our earnest wish that this program will be the beginning of an enlightenment which will enable our Governments to create an atmosphere which will enable the United States and Russia to live in Peace.'"[15]

The possibility of two-way exchanges generated offers and prompted much Dance Panel discussion. Lincoln Kirstein, general director of the New York City Ballet and a Panel member, received an offer from the Soviet Minister of Culture, inviting the company to perform in four Soviet cities in 1958. Kirstein's reactions are recorded in the Panel minutes for October 1956: "The Russian offer presents problems as George Balanchine is anti-Stalinist, and he thinks he might encounter difficulties if he appears in Russia. Therefore he personally does not want to go."

The idea of the New York City Ballet going to Russia came up again in 1957. Kirstein once again stated that Balanchine was "violently anti-Russian." But this time he also brought up the issue of aesthetic differences between the New York City Ballet's productions—which tended to eschew narrative and spectacle—and those of the Bolshoi and Kirov companies—which laid great emphasis on both. Kirstein said that "they would be criticized for their lack of scenery and costumes, and for the 'decadent music' they use. The effect of a wholly new vision and sound might appear very peculiar to the Russians."

By spring 1958 another American group was considered for Russian exchange—Jerome Robbins's Ballets: U.S.A., which was making its debut that summer at the first Festival of Two Worlds in Spoleto, Italy. The Dance Panel approved support for this company's tour of Europe and Israel from July to November 1959. The repertory included a piece by Todd Bolender, but the remaining repertory was by Robbins and included *Afternoon of a Faun*, *New York Export: Opus Jazz*, *Moves* (a ballet without music), and *Events*.

By 1958, Robbins was a well-known ballet and musical theater choreographer. Born in New York in 1918, he had studied both modern dance and ballet. At that time his credits included the ballets *Fancy Free* (1944), *Age of Anxiety* (1950), *The Cage* (1951), and *Afternoon of a Faun* (1953), and the musicals *On The Town* (1944), *High Button Shoes* (1947), *The King and I* (1951), and *West Side Story* (1957). Robbins had been a member of Ballet Theatre from 1940 to 1948 before joining the New York City Ballet in 1949 and becoming the company's Associate Artistic Director.

Members of the Moiseyev Dance Company in Soccer. *Dance Collection, The New York Public Library for the Performing Arts, Astor, Lenox, and Tilden Foundations.*

Robbins was quoted in the Dance Panel minutes as stating that the purpose of the company he had formed in 1958 was "to show Europeans the variety of techniques, styles, and theatrical approaches that are America's particular development in dance. Its repertory was chosen to extend from the classic ballet danced in tights, tutus, and toe shoes to our own current jazz style." The Russians turned down the offer of the Robbins company. They were not happy with bringing jazz to Russia, as it was considered a decadent Western form.

The Dance Panel had different priorities about what kind of dance should be sent to Russia. Emily Coleman, music and dance editor for *Newsweek*, said at the April 1959 meeting that she "has been involved in a study of Russian cultural exchange lately, and has reached the opinion that too much high-brow entertainment is being considered for Russia." Ann Barzel, the Chicago critic and dance historian, disagreed. She thought that "it was a mistake to send them popular entertainment alone; we should show them we have something good also." Martha Hill felt that "we should send the best musical comedy with the best jazz. The concept of ballet in our country and Russia differs."

A decision was finally made to send American Ballet Theatre (ABT) to the Soviet Union in 1960. ABT was to be the first American dance company sent to that country, and the question became whether we would best be represented by contemporary work, the traditional repertory, or a combination of the two. If only newer work were performed, some panelists argued, the Soviets would assume that the important classics were beyond our reach technically and artistically. On the other hand, if we brought only *Swan Lake* or *The Sleeping Beauty*, how would we show what was special about our view of dance?

The Panel was very concerned about the ballets that ABT would take to the Soviet Union and who would perform. At the November 1959 meeting, many questions were addressed to panelist Lucia Chase, who was also ABT's artistic director. Walter Terry wanted her to present cast and repertory to the Panel, "so that we can keep a careful eye on it." Chase responded that she would like to include *Fancy Free* and *Interplay* by Jerome Robbins; *Fall River Legend*, *Rodeo*, and *Tally-Ho* by Agnes de Mille; *Pillar of Fire* and *Jardin aux Lilas* by Antony Tudor; and *The Combat* by William Dollar. She wanted to do works that were not American, such as Fokine's *Les Sylphides*, which was also in the repertory of Soviet companies. She also wanted to bring along several dancers she considered to be stars, including Erik Bruhn, John Kriza, Scott Douglas, Royes Fernández, Lupe Serrano, Ruth Ann Koesun, Nora Kaye, and Violette Verdy.

The discussion about who would go to the Soviet Union with ABT continued at the February 1960 meeting. The minutes read: "Panel members want Miss Chase to have the finest company for Russia, and it was suggested that she ask Nora Kaye, Maria Tallchief, Alicia Alonso and Melissa Hayden." Chase noted that a new ballerina, Toni Lander, was joining the company—"who although Danish, is connected with no one nationality."

Agnes de Mille felt that the first American ballet company to go to the Soviet Union should include "everyone who owed his career to the Ballet Theatre and is a part of it." Lucia Chase wanted Agnes de Mille, Antony Tudor, and Jerome Robbins to rehearse their own ballets with the company, but only de Mille agreed to do this. The February minutes show that there was intense concern about putting the best foot forward. "After further discussion the Panel agreed that this is a national emergency and full cooperation of every dancer and every choreographer that Lucia Chase feels she needs must be urged."

Martha Hill moved that the State Department and the Dance Panel send letters to all choreographers whose works would be performed, requesting them to help with rehearsals. She also wanted letters sent to certain major dancers, including Melissa Hayden, Nora Kaye, and Maria Tallchief, asking them to join the company for the Soviet tour. Lucia Chase commented that there would be major problems with such a large number of stars. Who would be billed as first ballerina? Would there be enough repertory for all of them? Finally, it was moved that "the week before going to Russia be left free for all rehearsals, and that if necessary, the choreographers of each ballet to be done in Russia should be flown over to rehearse them." This was seconded and carried unanimously.

At the next meeting, in March, the Panel was informed that Rosamond Gilder, ANTA chairperson for the international exchange program, had written letters in the name of the Panel to Maria Tallchief, Melissa Hayden, and Nora Kaye, as well as to Antony Tudor and Jerome Robbins.

According to Lucia Chase, the letters "did neither harm nor good. Mr. Robbins gave one hour of rehearsal to the Company, which was invaluable, and Mr. Tudor has not helped at all. Miss Chase has talked with Maria Tallchief and believes she will come to Russia with the Company." Chase did not feel she would be successful in getting commitments from either Melissa Hayden or Nora Kaye.

The ABT tour of the Soviet Union lasted from September 13 until October 23. The repertory included two very "American" works. One was *Rodeo*, which had choreography by de Mille and music by Aaron Copland. The ballet was first produced in 1942 by the Ballet Russe de Monte Carlo and even today remains popular with audiences. It was original both in theme and movement; the story, about cowboys and cowgirls, included a square dance performed to hand-clapping. The other American work, originally created for Ballet Theatre, was *Fancy Free*. Choreographed in 1944 by Jerome Robbins to music by Leonard Bernstein, it portrayed three American sailors on shore leave, drinking, dancing, and flirting with three women.

The Dance Panel minutes of the November 1960 meeting contain a report on ABT's Soviet tour, based on comments by Lucia Chase:

> At the opening, Mme. Khrushchev, Mme. Ulanova, and all prominent choreographers were present and the performances went extremely well. The program consisted of *Theme and Variations*, *Rodeo*, *Black Swan*, and *Graduation Ball*. *Theme* was not liked as much as we thought it would be; *Rodeo* was received more enthusiastically than expected; the pas de deux almost brought down the house ("they had never seen a dancer like Erik Bruhn"); and *Graduation Ball* went well. The second program consisted of *Les Sylphides*, *Fancy Free*, *Don Quixote*, and *Bluebeard*. They liked *Bluebeard* and *Les Sylphides* the best.[16] The third program consisted of *Lady from the Sea*, *Combat*, *Jardin aux Lilas*, and *Theme and Variations*. *Combat* was an enormous success; Lupe Serrano was sensational in it. They were not sure of *Fancy Free* and Miss Chase feels this was the least successful; they did not feel it had a message. The Russians have great respect for our training; the American pirouette is faster, straighter, stronger than theirs; they also felt that our dancers had a stronger technique and better feet than theirs. However, they feel we do not use our arms as well.

Lupe Serrano in The Combat. *Dance Collection, The New York Public Library for the Performing Arts, Astor, Lenox, and Tilden Foundations.*

Maria Tallchief and Royes Fernández in Lady from the
Sea, *Soviet Union, 1960. Dance Collection, The New York
Public Library for the Performing Arts, Astor, Lenox, and Tilden
Foundations.*

At the November meeting Agnes de Mille questioned Chase as to why *Billy the Kid* and *Fall River Legend* were omitted from the Soviet programs. "Miss Chase said, regarding the former, it was thought by the Russians to be unsuitable because it made a hero out of an outlaw, and the Embassy suggested both be left out as both were too violent and too macabre for Russian taste." *Billy the Kid*, with choreography by Eugene Loring and music by Copland, was first produced in 1938 and quickly became a modern classic. It told the story of William Bonney, alias Billy the Kid, a notorious outlaw who was admired, feared, and finally shot by a sheriff who had been his friend. *Fall River Legend*, set to music by Morton Gould, was choreographed by de Mille in 1948. It was based on the infamous story of Lizzie Borden, who had killed both her father and stepmother with an ax.

Two of the ballets that were well-received were by Michel Fokine, who had left Russia in 1918 and spent his later years teaching and choreographing in the United States. *Les Sylphides* had premiered in Russia in 1908 as *Chopiniana*. Radical for its time, it was a plotless one-act ballet emphasizing feeling and flow rather than spectacle. The other Fokine ballet that Soviet audiences liked was *Bluebeard*, which treated the well-known story of Count Bluebeard and his seven wives in a somewhat lighthearted manner.

The Petipa classics were represented by the "Black Swan" pas de deux (usually performed by Tallchief and Bruhn) and the pas de deux from *Don Quixote*; George Balanchine by *Theme and Variations*, which he had choreographed for Ballet Theatre in 1947. Although the ballet had music by Tchaikovsky, the Soviet audiences were cool; it was plotless, a fantasy of pure classical movement. Antony Tudor's *Jardin aux Lilas* (1936), also known as *Lilac Garden*, was set to music by Ernest Chausson. A ballet of emotional subtlety set within a world of upper-class decorum and shifting appearances, it took place at a party on the eve of the heroine's marriage to a man she does not love.

The Combat (1949), inspired by Tasso's *Jerusalem Delivered* and choreographed by William Dollar, told the story of Tancredi, a Christian knight, and Clorinda, a Saracen girl. *Lady from the Sea* (1960), by Birgit Cullberg, took its theme from the play by Henrik Ibsen. A young girl plights her troth with a stranger who then disappears. After she marries another man and bears his children, the stranger returns—she rejects him: the romantic ideal has ceased to hold her in thrall. David Lichine's *Graduation Ball* (1940), to the music of Johann Strauss, was a lighthearted ballet set in old Vienna—a graduation party at a school for young ladies with cadets from a neighboring military academy. The climax of the ballet was a dance competition based on the fouetté, a virtuoso spinning step.

In her autobiography Maria Tallchief vividly recalls the Moscow performances during the 1960 ABT tour:

> To begin with, although it was September, the weather had turned cold. We were dancing not at the Bolshoi but at the Stanislavsky and Nemirovich-Danchenko Lyric Theater, a somewhat smaller house. It was freezing there, and nothing I did warmed me up. There was no heat backstage or in my dressing room, and when I tried to warm up I was so cold I couldn't feel my feet. It was the same when I went out on stage. The excitement of the occasion compensated for the primitive state of affairs we had to endure. Opening night the theater was packed. Two Soviet prima ballerinas, Galina Ulanova and Maya Plisetskaya, were in the audience, and all number of dancers, critics, and Soviet officials. Their eagerness and anticipation somehow conveyed themselves to us on stage.... After the performance, Ulanova and Plisetskaya came backstage to pay their respects, and hundreds of other people were hurling themselves at our feet.[17]

Erik Bruhn (left) and members of American Ballet Theatre look on as Maria Tallchief shakes hands with an admiring Soviet official, 1960. Dance Collection, The New York Public Library for the Performing Arts, Astor, Lenox, and Tilden Foundations.

Lucia Chase reported to the Panel that the Stanislavsky Theater seated 2,400 and was filled to capacity. The performances in Leningrad took place at the Theater of the Cultural Cooperative Center, which accommodated 2,100; the house was full for all programs. The company also performed in Tbilisi and in Kiev. Lucia Chase told the Panel that she felt the warmest audiences were in Leningrad and noted: "it was much freer and more like a Western city." The tour had started in Moscow, and the company returned there for the final performances. Chase reported that "many important people attended the last performance, including Premier Khrushchev, who invited seven of the Company to his box after the performance. Everyone asked them to come back and was most enthusiastic." Tallchief recalled Tbilisi, the capital of Georgia, as the highlight of the trip. "Audiences there were even more responsive than in the north, and I felt I danced better because of the sunny climate."[18]

Tallchief remembers always being watched. "As expected, our movements in the Soviet Union were closely monitored, and once we arrived, we were never permitted to go anywhere on our own. We ate together in one large group, and traveled everywhere by bus in what the Russians called a *delagatzie*. And at all times we were accompanied by a group of interpreters. They never once left our side." Sometimes police added to the human barricade, as during the Bolshoi performance of *Swan Lake*, when a twenty-two-year-old dancer from the Kirov by the name of Rudolf Nureyev, tried—unsuccessfully—to breach the wall and speak to his idol Erik Bruhn.[19]

Erik Bruhn. Photo by John Lindquist. Courtesy of the Harvard Theatre Collection, The Houghton Library.

Censorship and control were issues discussed by the Panel. Rosamond Gilder, the ANTA chair of the Dance Panel at that time, explained at the November 1960 meeting that "the performing arts are going to Russia on an international treaty or agreement.... This treaty gives us the right to refuse a company coming from Russia, either wholly or in part. Each country has the right of veto." Panelist Hyman Faine "reiterated that we should not again place ourselves in the position of being told what to do, if we think the decisions are wrong." Lucia Chase commented:

"The next time, if the Panel felt strongly about an American work, they could do it; it was not wise to fight for it the first time there."

The next company to appear in the Soviet Union under the international exchange agreement was the New York City Ballet. Lincoln Kirstein and George Balanchine were not overly enthusiastic about taking the company. Balanchine's view of the Soviet regime was extremely negative, as he had publicly stated on several occasions. In addition, Kirstein and Balanchine knew that accommodations, food, and performance conditions in the USSR would be poor.

There was considerable pressure from the State Department to send the New York City Ballet. The Soviets had already sent us two ballet companies. The Bolshoi Ballet came in April 1959, the Kirov Ballet in September 1961, and the Bolshoi returned in the fall of 1962. The success of ABT called for another American group of the highest caliber. According to the April 1962 minutes, Kirstein and Balanchine would go to the Soviet Union only if there were enough funding for the New York City Ballet to tour Western Europe also. This was solved with financial assistance from the impresario Sol Hurok, then in the midst of negotiations for the second U.S. Bolshoi tour. A note in the June minutes confirms that helping the New York City Ballet make its way to the Soviet Union was for Hurok "the only way he could secure the Bolshoi Ballet tour in America." Kirstein and Balanchine reluctantly agreed to an eight-week tour of the USSR in the autumn of 1962.

The company opened in Moscow on October 9 and gave its last performance in Baku on December 1; it also danced in Leningrad, Kiev, and Tbilisi. *The New York Times* dance critic John Martin accompanied the tour and filed a special report from Moscow on October 9. He pointed out that the troupe was the first American company to appear at the Bolshoi Theater, "and what is more important, it introduced a completely new style of ballet to its great stage." On opening night the audience saw Balanchine's *Serenade*, *Agon*, *Western Symphony*, and Robbins's *Interplay*. Martin commented: "A program of four short ballets, all without story, and three without scenery and costuming, is in marked contrast to the usual full evening of sumptuously produced ballets characteristic of the theater's regular procedure."

According to Lincoln Kirstein's account of the tour, there was a discrepancy between the reaction of the audience and what the Soviet newspapers wrote:

> While it was generally agreed (in private) that our training and equipment were "technically" accomplished, the concession was tempered by a tone implying that this quality was mechanistic, dictated by an impersonal, inhumane, or decadent formalistic servility. Our spareness in decoration and costume was hapless formalism; our androgynous lack of polarization between musculated males and bosomy females was the result of a fatal absence of Socialist health and psyche. Such was the verdict of a large por-

tion of printed opinion, yet certainly not of a vocative public which actually saw what we danced. Nor was it the judgment of that daring band of hopeless enthusiasts who followed our appearances from Leningrad to Tbilisi and Baku, back to Moscow and Kiev, who could hardly see enough of the novelty, strangeness, or freshness of a wholly alien vision and philosophy.[20]

John Martin was more specific in terms of the audience response to the different pieces on opening night. The first ballet on the program was Balanchine's *Serenade*, danced by Patricia Wilde, Allegra Kent, Jillana, Jonathan Watts, Nicolas Magallanes, and the corps. Martin wrote: "The Russian audience is an altogether honest one. It applauds furiously when it is moved to do so and it sits in absolute silence when it is not so moved. The evening opened in the latter mood. The first ballet...was beautifully danced....But the response was a perplexed and fairly indifferent one."

The next ballet on the program was *Interplay*, choreographed by Jerome Robbins and danced by Patricia McBride, Conrad Ludlow, and Anthony Blum in the solo roles. Martin reported that here "the atmosphere began to warm." *Agon*, a Balanchine-Stravinsky collaboration, followed; Martin wrote that the pas de deux, danced by Allegra Kent and Arthur Mitchell, "brought forth the first sign of genuine enthusiasm." In the weeks that followed the response to that pas de deux was overwhelming. "The Russian audience went wild over *Agon*, particularly the pas de deux," Allegra Kent recalled in her memoirs. "There had been no clues that it would be so well-received. It was a thrilling moment for me."[21]

Arthur Mitchell was African-American, and Kirstein described his performance as being "cool as spring water in its dispassionately erotic acrobatics....In the *Agon pas de deux* Balanchine had arranged one of his most ingenuous serpentine, linked patterns in equal balance between partners of opposite sexes."[22] Kirstein wrote that the Soviet press interpreted these patterns "as a Negro slave's submission to the tyranny of an ardent white mistress."[23] Whatever they may have thought, the audiences cheered, "Meech-elle, Meech-elle." For Allegra Kent, dancing the ballet in the Soviet Union gave a greater edge to their performing. "We walked out and posed in waiting silence until Robert Irving, our conductor, gave us the cue. Then I tore across the stage, spinning and lunging with Arthur behind me on the first fiery downhill diagonal, lunging and twirling recklessly. Stravinsky and Balanchine were back in Russia."[24]

Soviet audiences were delighted when the curtain rose on the last of the four ballets on the first program, Balanchine's *Western Symphony*. The painted backdrop, wrote Martin in his opening night report from Moscow, brought "a wave of heartfelt relief, for here at last was something that looked like a ballet. From there on, the temperature was high and in the final movement, which has been newly arranged by Balanchine, the show was stopped in its tracks by Gloria Govrin and, once again, by Mr. Mitchell."

ABOVE: *Allegra Kent and Arthur Mitchell in the* Agon *pas de deux. Martha Swope © TIME Inc.*

BELOW: *Edward Villella in the title role of* Prodigal Son. *Martha Swope © TIME Inc.*

The response had became more positive and enthusiastic. Martin felt that Balanchine had scored a victory. "At the final curtain Mr. Balanchine himself was the center of the greatest ovation, and he celebrated his first visit to his native country in nearly forty years in appropriate fashion." After opening night at the Bolshoi Theater, the company moved to the 6,000 seat Palace of Congresses,[25] where it played to sold-out houses. Before leaving Moscow for Leningrad on October 29, they returned to the Bolshoi Theater for six performances. Other ballets presented in the Soviet Union included *La Sonnambula*, *Symphony in C*, *Apollo*, and *Donizetti Variations*. Allegra Kent says that the Soviets did not want Balanchine's *Prodigal Son* because it was a Bible story, but he forced them to accept it. In addition to Kent and Mitchell, the New York City Ballet dancers who made the greatest impression on the Soviets were Edward Villella, Violette Verdy, Mimi Paul, Jacques d'Amboise, and Diana Adams (who performed only once because of an injury).

On October 20, while the company was dancing in Moscow, the Cuban missile crisis made headlines in the United States. Kirstein remembered: "The tension, indeed the terror, of those few days and nights, without a blow ever being struck in anger, were more demoralizing than anything I had ever encountered." He wrote that "the danger of our situation hardly percolated down to the dancers, who night after night within the Kremlin's walls heard six thousand voices yell for fifteen minutes after every performance: 'Bal-an-chin, Bal-an-chin!'"[26] Allegra Kent remembered it a little differently: the dancers were certainly aware of world events, but had a job to do. "The world looked as if it might blow up, but I couldn't miss a beat with my preparations for dancing or else I'd fall behind.... My muscles, mind, and shoes had to be ready because, despite the crisis, the audience didn't stay home."[27]

In his opening night *New York Times* article, Martin quoted two leading figures of the Soviet arts establishment as having certain reservations

about what they were seeing, although their general impression was positive. The ballerina Olga Lepechinskaya said: "Of course, we cannot accept everything we saw. There are things that are not very close to us." The composer Aram Khatchaturian said: "The only shortcoming of the American ballet troupe is the absence of a story line. But this shortcoming is made up by the brilliant technique of the artists."

The New York City Ballet in the Soviet Union, 1962. Front row seated *(from left): Allegra Kent, Edward Bigelow, Patricia McBride, John Taras, Jillana, William Weslow.* Second row seated: *Kay Mazzo (third from left), Karin von Aroldingen (sixth from left).* Middle row kneeling: *Arthur Mitchell (in striped T-shirt).* First row standing: *Balanchine (fourth from left), Diana Adams (in plaid robe), Sara Leland (in sweater), Earle Sieveling, Janet Villella, Edward Villella, Melissa Hayden (seventh, sixth, fifth, fourth from right).* Back row standing: *Jacques d'Amboise (in open-collar shirt), Robert Irving (in light jacket and tie). Courtesy of Edward Villella.*

Virginia Inness-Brown, former chair of ANTA's international exchange committee, gave a first-hand account of the tour when the Panel met on December 20. She had been in Moscow during the first week of performances, and corroborated Kirstein's observations that while the official press reaction was "cool," the public had responded very differently. She noted that performances were sold out and that "Mr. Balanchine and the artists were swamped with people following them and talking to them.... The reception for the Company was unique because the Bolshoi Ballet has a totally different kind of body movement than our ballet, and this was strange to them, but the tour was nevertheless successful."

At that same meeting, panelist Lillian Moore reported that she had received a twelve-page letter from a colleague in the Soviet Union: "She said [the company] was magnificently trained, with splendid artists who were superb. She was delighted that we had also sent the American Ballet Theatre so that they know that America does some other kind of dancing aside from Balanchine. They miss the story ballet.... As the performances progressed there was much better rapport between the audience and the dancers."

The Soviets provided their usual heavy surveillance, which meant that the company was supposed to stay together. As Kent wrote: "We had arrived in the land of group action." They had their meals in a special area in the dining room of the hotel and went everywhere with Intourist escorts. Kent "wondered what it would be like to work in a police state where citizens disappeared forever in the gulags."[28]

In Kiev, Shaun O'Brien, one of the dancers, did wander off and was arrested as he filmed scenes in a public park with an eight-millimeter camera. He was taken to a nearby building and held there for nearly five hours. The dancer explained that he did not speak Russian and wanted to call the hotel; he was not permitted to use the phone. For identification he showed his theater pass; he did not have his passport, which was being held at the hotel.

After a time an interpreter appeared, and O'Brien was questioned as to his intentions by officials in army uniform. They developed the film, and he was asked to sign a release for the film and what they called a "protocol"; he refused both requests. An individual from the Soviet central concert and touring bureau (Goskontsert) who had been assigned to the New York City Ballet finally showed up. He recognized O'Brien as a member of the company and urged him to sign the protocol, which he again refused. The developed film was produced, but could not be shown because there was no projector. O'Brien was finally released after he was assured that if there was nothing suspicious in the film, it would be returned with additional new film.

The following day, Hans Tuch of the USIA, who had been assigned by the Department of State to supervise the company during the tour, filed an official protest with Goskontsert. Tuch said the U.S. considered the

incident serious, viewing the long detention and general behavior of the
Soviets as unacceptable. The next day the film was returned to O'Brien
with an apology.[29]

Tuch sent a lengthy memorandum to the Department of State about
the tour. He had joined it on October 29, just as the company was finish-
ing its performances in Moscow. He traveled with it to Leningrad, where
the company performed through November 9; he also accompanied it to
Kiev (November 10–19), Tbilisi (November 20–26), and Baku (November
27–December 1). His report, dated December 3, was written while the
experience was still fresh:

> I believe that the New York City Ballet made a deep and lasting impres-
> sion on Soviet artists and intelligentsia who saw their performances and
> with whom they came into personal contact. This impact is not necessarily
> one that will make itself felt immediately. The volume and length of ova-
> tions increased to reach its zenith at the final performance in Leningrad
> when a rain of flowers showered onto the stage and the audience contin-
> ued its applause for over fifteen minutes after the final curtain.... The
> Soviets have long known about our magnificent symphony orchestras and
> our outstanding musical soloists, and they respect us for excellence in
> these fields. Ballet, however, they consider their own sphere.... No one
> has questioned Soviet superiority in ballet training, musicality and chore-
> ography. The New York City Ballet comes along and shows that in exact-
> ly these three vital areas of ballet their director and their dancers are supe-
> rior in many respects. This deep impression will translate itself into
> liberalizing further Soviet artistic efforts.... This, to my mind, is one of
> the long-range purposes of the cultural exchange program with the Soviet
> Union: to broaden the horizons of the Soviet intelligentsia and lead them
> toward individual expression and liberalization in thought.... I believe
> that the New York City Ballet deserves official recognition for its contri-
> bution to the U.S. objectives of the exchange program.[30]

The Dance Panel was interested in recommending another company
for the Soviet Union. The Robert Joffrey Ballet was approved in 1961 and
toured there from October to December 1963. Joffrey began studying
ballet in Seattle, where he was born in 1928. Moving to New York in
1948, he enrolled at the School of American Ballet, in addition to studying
modern dance. He did a considerable amount of teaching and also performed, sharing a number of concerts with May O'Donnell, a former
member of the Martha Graham company. His own company made its first
appearance on 29 May 1954 at the YMHA on Ninety-Second Street, a
venue closely associated with modern dance.

Joffrey was a new breed of ballet director. His emergence in the 1950s
signaled a new kind of ballet company on the American horizon—one in
which the emphasis was on contemporary choreography, with the standard nineteenth-century classics virtually eliminated from the repertory.
In the 1970s Joffrey was the first to invite postmodern choreographers

such as Twyla Tharp to create works for his company. In the 1950s and 1960s the repertory included such modern dance works as Alvin Ailey's *Feast of Ashes* and Anna Sokolow's *Opus '65*. Joffrey's company was small, young, ambitious, and modern.

The Dance Panel first discussed the Joffrey company in May 1960. "This company, consisting of 18 dancers in 11 ballets...was a small company with an excellent level of performance." It was decided to make every effort to see the company that summer at Jacob's Pillow in Massachusetts, where it would be performing. In January 1961 the Panel "felt [that the Joffrey company] should be added to the list of small classical ballet companies." The first tour made under government auspices was from December 1962 to March 1963 and took the Joffrey company to Jordan, Syria, Lebanon, Iraq, Iran, Afghanistan, India, and Egypt. The following October the company left for the Soviet Union.

The Joffrey Ballet went to the Soviet Union with a wide-ranging repertory. Five of the ballets were world premieres—Gerald Arpino's *The Palace*, Joffrey's *Gamelan*, E. Virginia Williams's *Patterns* (all by American choreographers), and two works by the English choreographer Brian Macdonald, *Caprice* and *Time Out of Mind*. The repertory also included Francisco Monción's *Pastorale*, August Bournonville's pas de deux from *Flower Festival in Genzano*, Ailey's *Feast of Ashes*, and Arpino's *Sea Shadow* and *Ropes*. Sasha Anawalt, in *The Joffrey Ballet*, writes: "The programs were loaded to give the Soviets their first experience with modern dance through Ailey's piece (restaged by him in a secular version without reference to Christianity and called in Russia *House of Sorrows*); their first exposure to the composer Charles Ives...whose score accompanied *Ropes*; and their first taste of Bournonville."[31]

Consisting of twenty-six dancers, the Joffrey company was small by Soviet standards. It was also very different from anything the Soviets had seen before. On opening night there were long ovations, which the company continued to receive throughout their tour. On November 22, while the company was in Kiev, it received the startling news of President Kennedy's assassination. Performances were canceled for three days by order of the American embassy, and Joffrey was able to obtain permission for a memorial service at St. Vladimir's Russian Orthodox Church.

From its inception, the Dance Panel had actively supported a particular vision of ballet, regarding this as a contemporary art form with a school of choreographers developed in America. For several years, from 1954 through 1958, the Panel had resisted endorsing the Ballet Russe de Monte Carlo, a company that represented an older, outdated emigré tradition.

The minutes for the December 1954 meeting read in part: "We are receiving requests for support of Mr. Denham's *BALLET RUSSE DE MONTE CARLO*. The Panel decided that this organization is inferior." There was no further discussion of the troupe until September 1956, when the minutes stated that the group was "not a representative American company" and that its "repertory had been dead for 20 years" (an uncredited remark that expressed what Lincoln Kirstein had been saying for years). The Ballet Russe de Monte Carlo was one of several companies that emerged in the 1930s after the demise of the celebrated ensemble founded in 1909 by Serge Diaghilev. Russian in origin, Diaghilev's Ballets Russes was Paris-based; its repertory of exciting new works—many of which became twentieth-century classics—offered music by Stravinsky and Ravel, designs by Picasso, Bakst, and Matisse, and choreography by modern masters, including Fokine, Massine, and Balanchine. None of the so-called international—or emigré—companies of the 1930s and 1940s displayed the spirit of adventure or consistently high standards of the earlier enterprise, even as they laid claim to its cosmopolitan identity.

During the 1950s, the Ballet Russe de Monte Carlo made its home in the United States. The company toured constantly, giving many audiences their first sight of ballet. However, the company had lost creative vigor. By the early 1950s it had ceased to produce new ballets and had lost many of its stars. Moreover, it had dropped virtually all its American works (many, interestingly, by women), including Agnes de Mille's *Rodeo*, Ruth Page's *Frankie and Johnny* and *Billy Sunday*, and Valerie Bettis's *Virginia Sampler*, produced in the 1940s. Heading the company was Sergei Denham, who had neither a strong artistic vision nor particularly good management skills.

Because of the weak indigenous tradition in America, most ballet teaching from the 1920s to the 1950s was done by Russian emigrés. Not all of them were equally gifted, but foreign origin gave them a definite cachet. When George Balanchine was brought to this country in 1933 by Lincoln Kirstein, he insisted on founding a school even before establishing a company in order to create a tradition of quality; the School of American Ballet and the New York City Ballet grew out of these efforts. Balanchine looked determinedly forward and from the start insisted on forming companies that used American trained dancers and rooting his choreography in American energies and ideas. When Ballet Theatre was founded in 1940, the goal was to form an American company with room both for new choreography and excellent productions of the traditional classics.

In evaluating the Monte Carlo group as nonrepresentative, members of the Dance Panel were in fact verifying the passing of an era in American dance when ballet was dominated by companies with roots in other soil. The political pressure brought to bear on the Panel was strong and potentially dangerous; the minutes of the December 1957 meeting record in detail the specifics. Robert W. Dowling, representing ANTA, had recently met with two of the most company's most powerful supporters: Julius Fleishmann, a businessman of great wealth (Fleishmann's Yeast) and president of a foundation that was one of the conduits for channeling CIA funds to the Congress for Cultural Freedom, and Watson Washburn, a well-placed lawyer:

Mr. Washburn informed Mr. Dowling that he was very angry at the treatment accorded the Ballet Russe. He said that if the Ballet Russe was not qualified by the Dance Panel of ANTA, he would destroy the entire President's program. Mr. Washburn claims he has connections in Washington to accomplish this. Mr. Dowling answered him by saying that such a statement is worse than saying you would destroy the whole missiles program if your designs were not accepted.... The Monte Carlo people are convinced they have a good company ... and they feel they are being discriminated against.

Ultimately, a committee of disinterested parties was appointed to write a short brief. The committee's mandate was to bring together all the objections voiced over the years against having this company represent America abroad. Dowling was concerned that "we must be able to prove we are entirely fair if we ever have to go before a Congressional Committee." Because of the way the Panel had addressed its task, it had ample ammunition to combat the pressure being brought against the program. Panelist Emily Coleman put it well: "In the building of any great project like the President's Program, there is bound to be someone against you.... We must meet this head on, and not let any group dominate or control the Government's cultural activities."

The Panel's handling of the Monte Carlo company was extremely fair. At the September 1956 meeting, it was decided to exclude Lucia Chase, Lincoln Kirstein, and Agnes de Mille "from making any decisions" on the project "because of their association with competing ballet companies." Also at that meeting, comments were made that "the Panel wishes to give [the company] every chance, therefore we should advise Mr. Denham that a committee from the Panel, excluding those who are involved or associated in any way with other ballet companies, will attend an audition or performance to see the repertoire and the Ballet's present standard of performance."

When it was announced at the October 1956 meeting that the Monte Carlo company would appear in Trenton, New Jersey, in November, a committee was appointed to attend the performance. The review was negative, and the Dance Panel decided it would rather support something "small and good, than big and bad.... The Company has no style, flavor, polish, etc." Panel members also attended performances during the company's spring 1957 season at the Metropolitan Opera House: once again, they voted for rejection. In January 1958 a report was under way. It enumerated the reasons for rejection: there was no premier danseur or prima ballerina; there had been no new repertory for twenty years; the scenery and costumes were shabby. Answering claims of popularity, sold-out houses, and good reviews on tour, the report noted the company's reliance on Community Concert Series subscriptions to sell tickets, unsophisticated audiences, and inexperienced critics.

Three ballet companies were sent to the Soviet Union—American Ballet Theatre, the New York City Ballet, and the Robert Joffrey Ballet. These companies were also sent to many other parts of the world, including South America, Europe and Asia. In addition, the San Francisco Ballet was sent to Asia (1957), South America (1958), and to the Middle East (1959). The Dance Panel was right to reject the Ballet Russe de Monte Carlo: it chose, instead, to give the world a vision of ballet that was contemporary, exciting, and made in the U.S.A.

The Foreign Service dispatch addressed to the State Department was dated 2 July 1962. It was from the American Embassy in Tokyo, and the subject was "Cultural Presentations: Report on de Lavallade-Ailey American Dance Company." The report was positive in tone: "de Lavallade-Ailey American Dance Company makes excellent impression in Japan.... Reviews excellent. Impact of performances on critics, dancers, theatre arts writers exceeded all expectations."[1]

The company, headed by Carmen de Lavallade and Alvin Ailey, was the first African-American dance group sent abroad under the sponsorship of the International Exchange Program. The dancers were young and talented; Ailey himself was only thirty-one. They had left the United States on January 30 and arrived in Sydney, Australia, on February 1, opening in that city two days later. Performances in Melbourne and Canberra were followed by stints in Burma, Vietnam, Malaya, Indonesia, the Philippines, Hong Kong, Formosa, Japan, and Korea. With sixty performances in twenty-five cities, the company was seen by 146,791 people before it left the Far East on May 3 and returned home.

Alvin Ailey in Rite. *Photo by Zachary Freyman. Dance Collection, The New York Public Library for the Performing Arts, Astor, Lenox, and Tilden Foundations.*

Sending African-American artists abroad became increasingly important as the civil rights movement grew and captured headlines. The world watched as the struggle unfolded. In 1955 the arrest of Rosa Parks sparked the Montgomery bus boycott. In 1957 Arkansas Governor Orval Faubus called out the state's National Guard to prevent court-ordered integration of Little Rock High School, and President Eisenhower dispatched federal troops to Little Rock. In 1961 mobs in Montgomery, Alabama, attacked black and white "Freedom Riders" who had entered the city by bus to test segregation barriers in interstate buses and terminals. And then in 1963 the world heard Martin Luther King, Jr.'s "I have a dream" speech at the Lincoln Memorial in Washington. His eloquent words heralded a message of freedom and opportunity for black and white, side by side.

Alvin Ailey, when speaking of his company's 1962 Asian audiences, observed that "most of what they knew regarding the U.S. Negro previously was negative. They all knew about Little Rock and the Freedom Riders."[2] Based on what is recorded in the Dance Panel minutes, there was no specific pressure from the State Department, the USIA, or ANTA to include black artists, nor was there any pressure from particular Panel members. What seems to have prompted the inclusion of African-American artists in the program was a growing awareness of their importance and the importance of their heritage to American dance.

In his autobiography, Ailey speaks bitterly about the racism of the decades when he came to maturity: "In the 1940s and 1950s the American dance world practiced a pervasive racism. For a variety of reasons: Our feet weren't shaped right, our butts were too big, our legs wouldn't turn out correctly.... The people who ran the major and minor ballet and modern dance companies coldly rejected, and broke the hearts of, many aspiring young black dancers."[3]

The modern dance world was on the whole more open to black dancers than ballet. Lester Horton in Los Angeles and Martha Graham in New York had black artists in their companies in the 1940s and 1950s, as did Anna Sokolow and Sophie Maslow. The New Dance Group, a product of the social protest and workers' movements of the 1930s, was another venue where black dancers could study and perform. However, Broadway, which employed numerous under-employed modern dancers, was pretty much segregated despite its liberal record in resisting McCarthyism. Blacks could dance in black shows like *House of Flowers* (in which both Ailey and de Lavallade made their New York debut), but not in shows like *My Fair Lady* or *Subways are for Sleeping*.[4] Race-blind casting lay in the future.

In Alvin Ailey the Panel had found an artist who used the modern dance vocabulary to speak about his heritage; he also created dances unrelated to it. Ailey was a charismatic performer, a passionate and compelling speaker and, at his best, an original and moving choreographer. He shared his March 1958 choreographic debut at the Ninety-Second Street Y with Ernest Parham, and the *Dance Magazine* review by Doris Hering gave Ailey most of the space and the praise. "As a dancer, Mr. Ailey is exceptional. He reminds one of a caged lion full of lashing power that he can contain or release at will. And perhaps because he is so unusual, he knows instinctively how to compose for other unusual dancers."[5] In December 1958, he presented a full evening of dances, with Carmen de Lavallade as guest artist. The review in *Dance Observer* noted: "The excellent company gave a rousing performance with outstanding portrayals."[6] Both reviews expressed some doubts about his choreography. Wrote Hering in her review of Ailey's shared concert with Parham:

> Sleek bodies sailing mermaid-like across the stage—high attitude turns—bumps and grinds—laugher and petulance and fantasy and sometimes falsity. All of these whirled in a welter of color and ruffles and dazzle throughout a long, ambitious performance. But every so often, just as the dazzle made us feel as though we were being tossed about inside a kaleidoscope, a moment of purity would emerge—pure humor, pure dance, or pure emotion. These moments made the concert worthwhile.[7]

Reviewing the December concert for *Dance Observer*, Harry Bernstein had mixed feelings about the new works, *Cinco Latinos* and *Ariette Oubliée*, but noted with satisfaction the improvements Ailey had made in *Blues Suite*:

> *Cinco Latinos (Five Dances on Latin Themes)*, is, more or less, a curtain raiser frankly intended to entertain....In the second work of the program, *Ariette Oubliée,* Mr. Ailey abandoned ethnic sources and chose for his ideograph some lines from Verlaine....This ballet, although not completely realized, nevertheless had some highly enchanting moments of fantasy....A second viewing of the *Blues Suite* showed it to be much more taut and integrated than at its first performance last year.[8]

Carmen de Lavallade appeared with the company as a guest artist. The other dancers were Ailey, Charles Moore, Jacqueline Walcott, Audrey Mason, Don Price, Claude Thompson, and Nancy Redi. *Dance Observer* praised the dancers: "Mr. Ailey has assembled a company of dancers that are versatile and energetic, and who delineate his choreography with great enthusiasm and theatricality."[9]

Although the Ailey company generated interest right from the start, it was not immediately given support. The December 1958 minutes described the group as "an all-Negro company which desires to tour Africa....The Company is appearing at the YMHA on Sunday, December 21st, and an effort will be made to get Panel members to see the performances." However, at the January meeting the Panel decided that the company was not quite ready for export: "Mr. Terry saw this performance and, while Mr. Ailey is a good dancer, and they do a blues number which is good, the troupe is not qualified for export at this time. Therefore the project is not approved."[10] A similar view was expressed at the November 1959 meeting:

> A European impresario is requesting transportation to get this company to Europe where she can set up a tour. Mr. Kirstein and Mr. Terry are familiar with it and feel it is not representative of the United States. Mr. Ailey is a good dancer, but his company has only one good number, and is therefore not considered ready for use under the President's Program. This was agreed unanimously. Mr. Kirstein said Mr. Menotti wants to

organize a Negro dance company for Spoleto next summer, composed of Geoffrey Holder, Talley Beatty, Louis Johnson, among others. This project would need a good organizer.

No one materialized to organize such a group, and at the February 1960 meeting, Panel discussion returned to the Ailey company:

> Although this has been turned down for use by our program, Claude Planson, Director of the Paris International Drama Festival, has asked if he might include the company as a representative of American dance this year. Should the Embassy encourage Planson to accept Alvin Ailey? This would be for approval without the use of Government funds. Miss Coleman said we do not like to interfere with someone being hired. The Panel, however, was of the opinion that this Dance Company was not of the calibre to bear any designation as the official representation from the United States. It was moved, seconded and carried not to recommend the Alvin Ailey Dance Company as a representative of American dance at the Festival.

The following year witnessed a dramatic change of opinion. The comments in the September 1961 minutes were most enthusiastic. "Alvin Ailey and Carmen de Lavallade and Company: the Panel was most enthusiastic about this attraction, and would recommend them to go anywhere." The panelists who had seen the company perform at Jacob's Pillow in late June and early July had very specific recommendations about programming and repertory:

> There were eight dancers in the Company at Jacob's Pillow. The Panel members felt that the dance "Roots of the Blues" was one of the most brilliant they had seen. They used tapes at Jacob's Pillow, and these were fine. It is a very exciting, very theatrical program, an all-Negro company, most dependable and disciplined, highly professional, and could be sent anywhere. Miss Pimsleur, the manager, should be told the weakest numbers, "Gillespiana" and "Knoxville," should not be included, but "The Roots of the Blues," "Portrait of Billie," "Revelations," and "The Beloved" would make an especially fine program. Mr. Faine moved the project be approved, and the programs will be submitted before finalizing anything. This was seconded and carried unanimously.

There were several reasons for the dramatic shift in the Panel's view of the Ailey company—Ailey's growing maturity as a choreographer, the strength and cohesiveness of his company as a performing ensemble, an awareness that African-American work needed to be seen abroad, the increasing acceptability of an all-black modern dance company. Ailey himself was becoming increasingly visible. He did a revue called *African Holiday* at the Apollo Theatre. He choreographed *Mistress and Manservant*, a dance version of Strindberg's play *Miss Julie*, and summer productions of *Jamaica* and *Carmen Jones*, and premiered what was to become—

and remains today—his company's signature piece, *Revelations*. Ailey was also in demand as a performer. In June 1961, he and Carmen de Lavallade danced *Roots of the Blues* at the Tenth Annual Boston Arts Festival. They repeated their success in July at New York's Lewisohn Stadium, a large outdoor amphitheater near City College that no longer exists. In addition, Ailey and his company were invited back to Jacob's Pillow, and once again they scored a resounding success.

The minutes for the October 1961 meeting indicate the panelists' concern about what would be included in the company's touring repertory. "CARMEN DE LAVALLADE-ALVIN AILEY AMERICAN DANCE COMPANY: Since their approval at the last meeting, the Department has decided to send them on a Far Eastern tour starting early 1962. They have submitted two program possibilities which were fully discussed." The first program was to consist of *Modern Jazz Suite*, *Roots of the Blues*, *Creation of the World*, and *The Beloved*. The panelists had only one problem with this program—the title of the piece *Creation of the World*. "From the program notes describing the dance, Panel members remembered it as *Letter to a Beloved*. Since Mr. Ailey has another dance on the program entitled *The Beloved*, they suggested that we ask Mr. Ailey to call this *Letter to a Lady*. They felt that *Creation of the World* is too pretentious and misleading a title, and not appropriate for the dance itself."

Ailey had planned to include six dances on the second program— *Cinco Latinos*, *Letter to a Beloved*, *Come Sunday*, *To José Clemente Orozco*, *Portrait of Billie*, and *Blues Suite*. Like the first program, this one lasted ninety minutes, which the Panel felt was too long. They suggested eliminating *Blues Suite*, as it was thirty-five minutes long and similar to *Roots of the Blues*. They also suggested cutting *To José Clemente Orozco*, a work choreographed by Ailey's mentor, Lester Horton, that was inspired by the revolutionary Mexican muralist. Although not explicitly anticapitalist, Horton's dance celebrated the poor and downtrodden Mexican peasant. Horton himself, while never a member of the Communist Party, had been accused of leftist leanings during the 1950s.

It was not unusual for the Dance Panel to review repertory and make suggestions; it did this for American Ballet Theatre and the New York City Ballet, among others. Ailey himself came to the December 1961 meeting to discuss the programs he would be taking abroad. He told the panelists that he was revising his plans, and hoped to create one-and-a-half programs based on American folk music. His new piece, *Been Here and Gone*, would be a curtain raiser for the first program. "In this work", he told the Panel, "Brother John Sellers, folk-singer, will represent all of the folk-singers of the country, wandering along, singing sea-chanties, lullabies, ring games, etc. It will be a light number. The pattern and structure will be a suite and will make the point of the similarity of folk dances all over the world." The remainder of the first program would consist of *The Beloved*, *Gillespiana*, *Roots of the Blues*, and *Letter to a Lady*, a solo choreographed by John Butler for Carmen de Lavallade, and *Revelations*.

The second program would consist of *Cinco Latinos*, *The Beloved*, *Adam in the Garden* (as *Creation of the World* was now renamed), *Roots of the Blues*, *Letter to a Lady*, and *Revelations*. Lillian Moore asked Ailey why he wasn't taking his new solo work to the *Hermit Songs* of Samuel Barber. According to the minutes, he responded that "it would not be interesting enough, but Panel members disagreed and suggested that he take it with him and try it out in some places. It is ready, easily carried, and would be a good addition to the program." The meeting ended with Ailey inviting the Panel to see the two programs either at the McCarter Theater in Princeton or at the YWCA's Clark Center in New York, where they would be tried out during the last week of January—just before the company's departure.

On January 30 the ten dancers and four musicians of the de Lavallade-Ailey American Dance Company boarded a plane for Sydney, Australia. In addition to de Lavallade and Ailey, the dancers were James Truitte, Minnie Marshall, Ella Thompson, Charles Moore, Thelma Hill, Don Martin, Georgia Collins, and Connie Greco, who was white. The four musicians were Les Grinage (bass), Bruce Langhorne (guitar), Horace Arnold (percussion), and folk singer Brother John Sellers.

The Alvin Ailey company in Revelations, Southeast Asia, *1962. Photo by Dick Campbell. Courtesy of Dick and Beryl Campbell.*

Been Here and Gone was danced to traditional black music sung by Brother John Sellers and Ella Thompson. Ailey's program note[11] explained what he felt it important for audiences to understand: "The folk bards of the American South wandered in and out of the towns and cities, creating and carrying their songs of life's joys and sorrows and then disappearing into the country night—mostly unknown and unrecognized.... Among these men have been Huddie Ledbetter (Leadbelly), Blind Lemon Jefferson, Big Bill Broonzy." For Lester Horton's *The Beloved* the note was brief: "Out of an era of servility and dogma comes a theme of fanatic bigotry leading to violence." Ailey's *Two for Now—Modern Jazz Suite* had a simple note: "Two lyric dances exploring the inter-relationship between modern jazz music and its influence on the contemporary dance idiom." *Roots of the Blues*, with traditional music arranged by Sellers, offered a short explanation of the blues: "From the fields, levees and barrelhouses of the Southern Negro sprang the Blues—hymns to the secular regions of his soul." Ailey's *Revelations*, set to spirituals arranged by Howard Roberts, merited a longer explanation: "This suite explores motivations and emotions of Negro religious music, which like its heir the blues, takes many forms—true spirituals with their sustained melodies, song-sermons, gospel songs and holy-blues... songs of trouble, of love, of deliverance." Glen Tetley's *Mountain Way Chant*, which had music by Carlos Chávez, was "an archaic ritual of the Navaho Indian."[12]

Thelma Hill (left), Alvin Ailey, Carmen de Lavallade, and Brother John Sellers taking a curtain call during the Southeast Asia tour. Photo by Dick Campbell. Courtesy of Dick and Beryl Campbell.

The company was a huge success. The July 2 report from the American Embassy in Japan to the Department of State included reviews that ranged from the exuberant to the ecstatic.[13] "Is it really possible, I was asking myself, that I feel so elated and beautified by seeing a dance? I was leaving the theatre after the show was over, my heart still dancing with your rhythms that fly toward the future, my head deep in thought" (*Ongaku Buyo Shimbun*). "The dancing on the stage, as the program went on, demolished the barriers between countries, forced us to forget all the stuff about race, color, creed, etc. and embraced the house in a tight arm in arm hold between dancers and audience" (*Tokyo Shimbun*). "There is nothing more American than American Negro music, which, being the basis of jazz, has stamped a deep mark upon the music of today.... Their dance numbers, though thematically different, all conveyed the soul of Negro art, the joys and sorrows of a suppressed race, with vivid modern sensitivity.... We heartily admire the mastery of technique, the amplitude of expression, and the free, easy, unbridled bodily movements of the dancers including above all, de Lavallade and Ailey" (*Asahi Shimbun*).

A foreign service dispatch, signed by William C. Trueheart, Counselor of the American Embassy in Saigon, gave a long review of the de Lavallade-Ailey visit that began on March 2 and ended on March 8.[14] Trueheart was extremely positive about the season and the response of the audience: "The visit of this dance company in Vietnam marked the introduction of a completely new form of artistic presentation to the Vietnamese.... There were enthusiastic 'ohs' and 'ahs' when the curtain went up—surprise and delight at the stage sets and costuming. And as each performance progressed, there was more real appreciation for the excellence of the dancing itself."

Ailey responding to questions during the Southeast Asia tour. Photo by Dick Campbell. Courtesy of Dick and Beryl Campbell.

Trueheart also enthused about the way the dancers mingled with a variety of people and their genuine interest in Vietnamese music and dance:

> In all of their contacts with the Vietnamese, the dancers showed sensitivity to a culture that was new to them and genuine interest in the people themselves. The day after their arrival, USIS held a press conference for the leads. Alvin Ailey gave an inspired—almost evangelistic—explanation of the modern American dance and gave the newsmen a chance to question him on details. The group, almost in toto, accepted the invitation of a Chinese music group to attend a song and dance performance arranged especially for them. And Miss de Lavallade and Mr. Ailey met with a group of students and the Public Affairs Officer for a discussion of the dance and youth.

It is interesting that nowhere in the report from Saigon is there any mention of the fact that this was a group of African-American dancers with a repertory consisting of several "ethnic" works. As Trueheart's report makes clear, the dancers were accepted as Americans: "The dancers represented admirably not only their own field but the United States in general." Trueheart was very pleased that "the Vietnamese could meet artists who are such outstanding *people*—sensitive, charming, and gracious." Last but not least, neither he nor his colleagues "had ever seen a traveling group of entertainers more seriously dedicated to their profession and what they had to offer." In 1967, when the Ailey company returned to Africa, visiting Ethiopia, Malagasy Republic, Uganda, Kenya,

Tanzania, Congo, Ghana, Ivory Coast, and Senegal, it again received rave reviews.

From 1954 through 1961 the Dance Panel discussed four other African-American artists whose choreography had strong roots in American modern dance—Janet Collins, Katherine Dunham, Pearl Primus, and Donald McKayle. At the December 1954 meeting the name of Janet Collins came up. She was a cousin of Carmen de Lavallade and had grown up in Los Angeles; one of her main teachers was Lester Horton, Ailey's early mentor. Collins made her New York debut in 1949 at the Ninety-Second Street Y and was the first African-American hired as premiere danseuse at the Metropolitan Opera, where she performed from 1951 to 1954. According to the minutes, she "did not want to be received solely as a Negro dancer." A very gifted artist, Collins had a reputation for being erratic. Alvin Ailey, in his autobiography, described her as "a fantastic artist.... But she had psychological problems that later drove her to religious extremes and out of the dance world."[15] The Panel concluded that Collins was "temperamental and a slow choreographer.... Unless she presents some wonderful plans for herself, she would not be acceptable with her own company."

Katherine Dunham was the second African-American artist considered for touring support. Her name first came up in 1955; over the next three years discussion of her case embroiled the Panel in controversy. Born and raised in Chicago, Dunham exploded on the dance scene in the 1930s. She started a school and company, received a prestigious Rosenwald Travel Fellowship to study dance in the West Indies, and received a bachelor's degree from the University of Chicago. She danced at the Chicago Civic Opera and the Chicago World's Fair, choreographed *Primitive Rhythms* (1937), *Haitian Suite* (1937), and *Run, Little Chillun!* (1938). In 1939 she came to New York, where she staged the "Bertha and the Sewing-Machine Girl" number for the second edition of *Pins and Needles*, and choreographed *Tropics and "Le Jazz Hot"*, which opened at the Windsor Theatre early the following year.

Dunham pursued a wide variety of projects during the 1940s. In 1940 she appeared with her company in the Broadway musical *Cabin in the Sky*, which was

Katherine Dunham in L'Ag'ya, *1940s. Courtesy of Katherine Dunham. Missouri Historical Society.*

staged by George Balanchine. She choreographed several Broadway shows, including *Tropical Revue* (1943), *Carib Song* (1945), and *Bal Nègre*, which opened at the Belasco in 1946 and then toured nationally and internationally. She also made movies: *Star Spangled Rhythm* and *Pardon My Sarong* (both 1942) and *Stormy Weather* (1943), among others.

In 1945 she opened the Dunham School of Dance and Theater in New York; within two years, it had an enrollment of 350 students.[16] During the late 1930s and 1940s she created many important works: *L'Ag'Ya* (1937), *Plantation Dances* (1938), *Rara Tonga* (1942), *Choros* and *Rites de Passage* (both 1943), and *Shango* (1945). Between 1945 and 1947 she toured *Caribbean Rhapsody* with her company in Mexico and Europe. Somehow, she found time to write several articles and her first book, *Journey to Accompong*, which was published in 1946.[17]

She choreographed *Southland*, one of her most controversial dance works, in January 1951; the subject, she felt, explained the lack of later support from the international exchange program and the State Department. Commissioned by the Symphony of Chile, *Southland* premiered at the Opera House in Santiago. It was an angry and confrontational ballet about lynching. In the program notes Dunham wrote: "This is the story of no actual lynching in the southern states of America, and still it is the story of every one of them."[18]

In the opening scene, a chorus of singers stands in front of an antebellum mansion. The focus shifts to a duet for two black lovers, Lucy and Richard, followed by a contrasting duet for a white couple, Julie and Lenwood, who are drunk. Julie is beaten viciously by Lenwood, and left unconscious. A group of field hands, including Richard, discover her; after they leave, Richard lifts Julie's head to see if she is alright. Opening her eyes, she accuses him of raping her—and calls him "Nigger."

Richard is lynched, and his body swings by the neck from a magnolia tree. Joined by Lucy, the chorus becomes a cortège of mourners. The final scene, set in a cafe, shows couples dancing while men gamble and a blind man begs. Julie's funeral cortège appears. The dance ends on a note of hopelessness, a feeling of unresolved hatred and racism. "For a moment everyone is motionless. Then cards fall from the hands of a gambler, a woman weeps silently and couples tighten their embrace to grind slowly...while a man slowly opens his knife and continues to plunge it into the floor.... The blind man suddenly stands straight up. 'Seeing' what the others feel but cannot define, he follows the funeral procession."[19]

The response from the American Embassy in Santiago was extremely negative. Although a few days remained of Dunham's engagement, *Southland* was absent from the programs. It was next given at the Palais de Chaillot in Paris in January 1953. Reactions were mixed:

> There were praises by the French Communist newspaper *L'Humanité*...and complaints by the conservative *Le Monde*....While *Southland* marshalled criticism from radio commentators, who advised Dunham not to show blacks hanging on the stage, several of the Communist newspa-

pers felt she hadn't gone far enough to show her anger and wanted to see the burning of the body on stage.[20]

Southland was never performed again, but Dunham felt its repercussions long afterward. When she opened in Montevideo in 1954, she found that her impresario had booked José Limón to open on the same evening. Limón was there on a government-sponsored tour, while Dunham was there as an independent artist. The American Embassy hosted a cocktail party for Limón, but did not invite Dunham.

There is no evidence that the State Department or the U.S. Embassy had a hand in scheduling the overlapping premieres. Limón's booking was done at the last minute, and it is more than likely that the foreign service people stationed in Montevideo were not only unaware that Dunham was performing, but did not even know who she was. The final straw for Dunham, as she recalls, was that the impresario was told to go to Limón's opening night and not to hers.

Katherine Dunham in a publicity still, 1940s. Dance Collection, The New York Public Library for the Performing Arts, Astor, Lenox, and Tilden Foundations.

Beginning in 1955, the Dance Panel showed great interest in Dunham. Indeed, there is no indication that *Southland* detracted from the Panel's support of her or that the State Department exerted pressure against her. There is, however, a cryptic note in the minutes of the September 1955 meeting: "We should try to approach her again."

There is no earlier mention in the minutes of when or how Dunham was approached. Involved in many projects, Dunham toured extensively in the 1950s, mostly abroad. By the end of 1954 she felt compelled to close her New York school because, in addition to financial problems, she had not been able to give it her full attention. In late November 1955 she and her company began a four-week run at New York's Broadway Theatre.

Following engagements in Australia, New Zealand, and the Far East in 1956 and 1957, Dunham disbanded her company. She remained in Japan to complete the first volume of her autobiography, *A Touch of Innocence*; the writing was interspersed with work on two films—*Green Mansions* (U.S.A., 1958) and *Karaibishe Rhythmen* (Austria, 1960). It was not until

1962 that Dunham was back in New York at the Fifty-Fourth Street Theatre with her revue *Bamboche*. One of Dunham's biographers, Terry Harnan, notes the many challenges she faced during the 1950s—arthritis and
knee problems that curtailed her own performing; the adoption of a
daughter in 1951; separation from her husband, John Pratt; problems with
IRS about back taxes; increased emotional and financial stress because of
constant traveling.[21]

Dunham herself recalled that in December 1955 the Dance Panel had
suggested to her that a South American tour might be arranged. Dunham
did not think too highly of the suggestion: "We had just returned from
our second extended tour of South America and I felt a return to that area
at that time would have been devastating."[22]

In an interview with *International Variety* in May 1958, Dunham
expressed great anger with ANTA and the State Department for not providing government support for any of her tours. "The State Department
has given us no recognition whatsoever, and it is becoming increasingly
difficult for me in giving interviews to canny press people to cover up for
what could look like discrimination to the rest of the world."[23]

The Dance Panel discussed the *Variety* article at the August meeting.
"We have not heard from Miss Dunham directly, but should she present
herself again, we wish to know what action should be taken." There was
definitely mixed feeling about the quality of her work at this time. One
comment, not attributed to any particular individual, indicates the general
esteem she commanded: "Miss Dunham is a great artist and a great showman, and should be given the fullest consideration." Emily Coleman felt
that "we must see the show she has in mind. Columbia Concerts is planning a South American tour for her, and wants to know if there is any
possibility for assisting it." Another panelist expressed his unhappiness
with her recent work: "Mr. Frankenstein said the last time he saw her, she
had become theatrical in the cheapest sense. There was no authenticity; it
was night club material. He would hesitate before approving this without
seeing her again."

Dunham had long received mixed reviews from critics. Some argued
that she was chiefly catering to popular taste and producing cheap entertainment; others that she was a serious artist and anthropologist.[24] Dunham's work covered a wide range—from night club and movie work to
more serious choreography that integrated her anthropological studies.

At the August 1958 meeting the Dance Panel summarized its views on
Dunham: "In case further correspondence comes in, the Panel is perfectly
open to considering her troupe if she has a program along the lines of her
early work, but they are not interested in purely theatrical performances.
If she is having a performance in New York, the Panel will welcome an
opportunity to see her since they have not done so in recent seasons."

After extended discussion at the meeting on May 1959 meeting, Dunham was approved for government export. Dunham had submitted to the
Panel a number of program ideas in addition to repertory she was then

performing. "She has opened in Glasgow, but the reviews are unknown at this time. Her programs were read in toto; they show what the American Negro has arrived at today through showing the different influences which have determined the dances of today." Panelist Walter Terry, who was not present at the meeting, "called to report that he spoke with a person who attended this opening who said 'it was not brilliant.'"

Panelist Agnes de Mille felt that the problem with Dunham was that "the quality of her work varies from time to time." Another panelist noted that Dunham "was a remarkable and subtle artist, but had become something more of a 'Mistinguette' personality." A third urged the Panel to endorse her: "Miss Dunham is a great theater person, the first artistically serious Negro dancer in America, and most worthy of serious consideration." The final decision was to "tentatively approve Miss Dunham as a theatrical performer for an extension from Europe into Africa."

There are no heroes or villains in the Dunham episode. The Panel's concern about the erratic quality of her work was certainly not unjustified. She did not consistently pursue her requests to them, and for long periods of time in the 1950s she had little contact with the United States. In retrospect, perhaps both sides could have acted more vigorously. When approved in 1959 Dunham did not have a company; the following year she formed one for a European tour. In 1966 she went to Africa as an individual artist under the government's Leaders and Specialists program.

The name of Pearl Primus first came up at the Panel's September 1955 meeting. Her story, as it relates to the international exchange program, is similar to Dunham's but less complicated and bitter. Primus, who died in 1994, was a major figure as a choreographer, anthropologist, and teacher. Born in 1919 in Trinidad, she created dances that integrated research on Africa with a passionate feeling for the heritage of African-Americans. She made her solo concert debut in 1944 in New York and was awarded a Julius Rosenwald Fellowship in 1948 to study dance in Africa.

Upon her return to the U.S. in late 1949, Primus gave many lecture demonstrations based on her findings in Africa. In late 1950 she formed a company that spent the next two years on tour in England, France, Israel, and West Africa. From 1953 to 1959 Primus danced and taught in the United States as well as in Trinidad, Italy, and Spain. In 1959 she was appointed Chairman of Cultural Activities and Director of the African Center of Performing Arts in Liberia. Her goal was the development of a preservation program for indigenous dance and the related arts, and she maintained her connection with this Center until 1961.

After another performing and teaching trip to Africa in 1962, Primus opened a school in New York. In 1968, with a grant from the U.S. Office of Education, she also worked in New York's elementary schools. In 1974 Ailey invited Primus to recreate *Fanga* and *Congolese Wedding*, two of her most famous dances, for his company. Primus completed her Ph.D. in anthropology in 1978 at New York University and proceeded to win many awards and honors, including a National Medal in the Arts (1991).

According to the minutes of the September 1955 meeting, Primus was then "working on her plan and will invite the Panel to a rehearsal when she has her new company organized." The December minutes noted: "The Panel commented on the special performance which she had given for them in November. In general they felt it was far too untheatrical, and the company was amateurish. Also, Miss Primus herself is about thirty pounds overweight. On this basis the project was not acceptable to the Panel."

By this time Primus had married Percival Borde, a dancer, choreographer, and teacher from Trinidad. Their son was born in 1956, and the whole family went to Liberia in 1959. In 1961 her name, along with that of Borde, came up, and this time the Panel was wholehearted in its support. "They wish to tour the countries of West and Central Africa not only 'to show the new states of Africa the dynamism of the Performing Arts, the scope of cultural development of the Negro in America, the immense importance of preserving every facet of our heritage in the formal presentation of the folk art of the Nation,' but also 'to learn from the African leaders...how the United States can assist in the cultural development of the African countries.'" Primus was approved; her work was cited as being "always of the highest cultural level." Although the Panel still thought she had "a weight problem," it noted that she could "still do all the dances in her repertory."

Primus and Borde never went abroad under the auspices of the International Exchange Program. In 1962 the Rebekah Harkness Foundation provided funds for Primus, Borde, and the musician Chief James Bey to give a series of intensive workshops and performances throughout West and Central Africa. The original plan called for a four-month tour, but this was extended to ten months as the threesome worked its way through Liberia, Ghana, Togo, Cameroon, Sierra Leone, Guinea, Mali, Ivory Coast, Nigeria, Southern Rhodesia, Kenya, Uganda, Burundi, and Dahomey.

Two reports from State Department personnel in the field shed interesting light on how Primus's work was received in Africa. The first, an airgram from the American Embassy in Cotonou, Benin, noted that "Miss Pearl Primus is visiting Dahomey once again, this time at the invitation of the President of the Republic, Hubert Maga....Miss Primus and her husband, Percival Borde, gave a dance recital in the President's garden to an invited audience of some 150 persons." The report included an English translation of a review published by the government's Information Service:

> Anyone who is anybody, socially or officially in Cotonou or Porto-Novo was invited Saturday night by the President to attend a dance festival by the American Negro dancer Pearl Primus....This artist has a most winning personality, for she makes of the dance not only a spellbinding and captivating show but a cult as well. She knows equally successfully how to

combine the African dances with those brought over to Brazil and the Antilles by our ancestors. To be sure, Mrs. Primus adds a bit of classical choreography which smacks a bit of the theatre, but it is all so amusing that no one could complain.... When Primus pounds the ground with her bare feet, never a gesture too many, no force, the body is possessed with a haunting rhythm, but stateliness is there throughout the dance.[25]

Primus was one of several artists mentioned in the second report, which discussed a number of performances given in Africa in the two-year period from 1961 to 1963.[26] "Pearl Primus gave the impression of showing Nigerians how African dances should be presented though this may not have been her objective. Her show is said to have been a very poor one." The author, a Counselor at the Embassy in Lagos, does not seem to have been particularly interested in the performing arts or knowledgeable about them. He ends with the following recommendations: "It is a mistake for American performers, even Negroes, to try to interpret African culture for Africans.... Circus type shows ... go over well with sophisticated and unsophisticated audiences."

Although these comments were not made in connection with the international exchange program, they indicate the kinds of problems that frequently arose with USIS and embassy officials abroad. Many neither knew nor cared about the American performing arts, had a limited cultural background, or were simply uninterested in helping government-sponsored artists. The judgments they relayed to the State Department could reflect ignorance and even prejudice; fortunately, the Panel system was strong enough to advance artistic opinions of greater merit.

One other African-American artist was approved by the Dance Panel in 1962— Donald McKayle. Born in 1930 in New York, he made a stunning choreographic debut in 1951 with *Games*, a work

Pearl Primus in Folk Dance, *1945. Photo by Gerda Peterich. Dance Collection, The New York Public Library for the Performing Arts, Astor, Lenox, and Tilden Foundations.*

utilizing African-American children's play songs. Other successful works followed, including *Her Name is Harriet* (1952), *Nocturne* (1953), and *Rainbow 'Round My Shoulder* (1959). A charismatic performer, McKayle was a member of Graham's company during her government-sponsored Asian tour in 1955.

McKayle's name first came up in 1958 when Doris Humphrey proposed touring a program featuring young artists. The idea of sending McKayle's company abroad was approved in December 1962. "It was agreed that Mr. McKayle is a gifted choreographer and director and has some qualities of value for the Program. He is a Negro leader of an inter-racial group.... It was agreed to keep Mr. McKayle on the approved list and when there is a chance of using him, the Panel will discuss his repertory and personnel." Some Panel members were enthusiastic about the company's recent appearances; others felt some of the newer work was "over-costumed and over-danced"; hence the proviso about reviewing his repertory.

Between 1954 and 1962 several African-American jazz and ballet groups were considered and, for a variety of reasons, rejected. Two were companies that no one on the Panel had seen—Ballet Jazz and the First Negro Classical Ballet. Another, the Negro Dance Theater, had temporarily disbanded. The New York Negro Ballet had expressed interest in being sponsored, but could offer no specific information as to repertory and company size. After viewing one of its performances, the Panel decided the group was unsuitable; the minutes give no explanation why.

In June 1957 the American Embassy in Rabat requested an opinion from the Dance Panel regarding the American Negro Ballet Jazz Group. The Panel's response was marked confidential: "For the purposes of the President's Program, the American Negro Ballet Jazz Group was turned down by the Dance Advisory Panel of ANTA; but the leader Archie Savage is considered a fine dancer, and although the Panel does not recommend the Embassy associate itself with the group officially, it would not like to have the local impresario be discouraged from booking it."

In its place, the Panel approved an intriguing project developed by the well-known jazz expert Marshall Stearns. This was a lecture-demonstration on the history of jazz dance, with Albert Minns and Leon James as featured artists. In October 1958 the entire Panel watched a rehearsal and made several recommendations: that two women be added, that costumes rather than street clothes be used, and that the whole be made more theatrical. The Panel's recommendation was passed on to the State Department, which informed the Panel that the project would not be financed for Europe, but only for an Africa-Middle East tour. Stearns, Minns, and James eventually took the project abroad under private sponsorship.

Survival for dancers is always difficult. For African-American artists of the 1950s it was especially so. Segregation, racial prejudice, and stereotypes about physical appearance all played a role in how these artists were able to support their work and their companies. The Dance Panel seems to have felt a commitment to sending abroad African-American artists, but issues of content and style arose when they considered work that was marginal to their experience and frequently inimical to their taste. Dunham often ran into trouble for the overt sexuality of her dances. As critic Margaret Lloyd wrote about a 1943 performance in Boston: "It sent the critics thumbing through their thesauruses for synonyms of 'torrid.' The pelvic girdles, and there were many of them, did indeed seem to be made of melted lastex."[27] Primus seemed less interested in exploiting her material for commercial purposes.

The one African-American dance tradition that the Panel utterly failed to appreciate was tap. Although several outstanding African-American tappers were dancing in the 1950s, there was no discussion of artists such as Honi Coles and Cholly Atkins who were famous for their "class acts." Although panelists were aware of African-American artists—such as Primus and Dunham—working in the concert field, they were not particularly interested in tap and did not see it as a serious art form.

Still, at some point the Panel felt the need to send a tap act abroad. Its choice fell on Georgie Tapps, a white tapper familiar to audiences from his appearances on television's *Toast of the Town*; in 1957 he received rave notices in London for the show *United Notions*, which he both choreographed and performed.

Tapps was born George Becker in New York, and received early training with Ned Wayburn, a Broadway dance director and teacher active from the turn of the century to the 1930s.[28] Tapps himself danced in vaudeville and on Broadway. He had followed Gene Kelly in *Pal Joey*, performed at the Radio City Music Hall, and done many nightclub engagements. In 1952 he wrote a series of articles for *Dance Magazine* on "The Basic Facts and Techniques of Tap Dancing."

The Panel sent Tapps and his company to Africa from December 1961 through April 1962. The tour began in Ghana, continued through West Africa, and eventually included thirteen countries—Togo, Dahomey, Nigeria, Congo, Rhodesia, Mozambique, Tanganika, Uganda, Kenya, Madagascar, Upper Volta, Mali, and Morocco. He traveled with four dancers, two musicians, and a stage manager.[29]

The program that Tapps presented abroad included dances to a medley of songs by Rodgers and Hammerstein, a solo to "Malagueña," a group number to "That Old Black Magic," and a soft shoe dance to "Swanee River." Another number featured American songs, dances, and costumes popular between 1900 and 1925; this number lasted eleven minutes and had sixteen costume changes. In Ghana, Tapps held a tap dance clinic for fifty people. When he returned to Ghana for a two-day layover, the local dancers demonstrated what they had learned. The next day, Tapps gave a second clinic in which he also taught something about various aspects of stagecraft.[30]

Missing from all this tap work was the improvisation, complex rhythms, and inspired sense of personal style typical of African-American tap. What Tapps was doing was white tap, closer to what was seen in movies, musicals, and tap studios all over the U.S. Apparently, the irony of sending a white tapper to Africa was lost on the members of the Panel.

Increasing interest and support for African-American artists by the Dance Panel has to be seen against the backdrop of the civil rights movement. The members of the Dance Panel knew the world was watching. They were nervous when they sent Alvin Ailey. He was talented, but also young. At some other point in history they might have made him wait for support. But external events were too powerful to ignore. And as the triumph of his company proved, the world was certainly ready for him.

I heard that you ask'd for something to prove this puzzle the New World,
And to define America, her athletic Democracy,
There I send you my poems that you behold in them what you wanted

—Walt Whitman, "To Foreign Lands," 1860

Whitman's "athletic Democracy" encompassed a broad spectrum of heritage and heredity, of hopes and dreams. In the 1950s the Dance Panel struggled with "this puzzle the New World," with its many colors, cultures, and religions.

The idea of sending a Native American group abroad was first mentioned at the meeting on 10 March 1955. Edward Magnum was one of two theater professionals hired by ANTA in 1954 to travel to the Middle and Far East and make surveys as to facilities, booking techniques, and interest in the performing arts. The minutes of the March meeting note: "There is a great deal of interest in the American Indian abroad, as Ed Mangum found out on his recent survey trip." The initial suggestion was to send a Native American group to the International Folk Music Festival in Oslo. The Music Panel had suggested the Dance Panel seek advice from Willard Rhodes, a Columbia University professor and ethnomusicologist, regarding who would be suitable for this Festival.

Nothing concrete followed from these suggestions, but at the next meeting on April 7 Walter Terry brought up the general idea of sending a Native American group. He recommended Reginald and Gladys Laubin and argued that although both were white, they were "great exponents on Indians." The Laubins had taken a group of Crow Indians to Europe, and Terry had the impression that "they had been a great success." They had lived among the Sioux, Crow, Cheyenne, and other Plains Indians, and had been adopted by the Sioux. The name of Tom Two Arrows (Thomas Dorsey) was also mentioned at this time; an Onandaga Indian of the Iroquois Nation, he performed dances as a soloist and was also a musician and a craftsman.

Mary Stewart French, representing the State Department, was present at the October 13 Dance Panel meeting. She reported that the Laubins had been "a success in the Middle East, but not in Western Europe. This may be because they are too civilized, and do not act according to the preconceived notion that Europeans have of American Indians." Finally, it was Tom Two Arrows who was sent to Asia and the Far East (Pakistan,

Tom Two Arrows. Photo by John Lindquist.
Courtesy of the Harvard Theatre Collection,
The Houghton Library.

Burma, India, and Indonesia). Fully funded by the exchange program at $14,000, he did not have to supplement his income with commercial bookings.

Tom Two Arrows went abroad for four months in 1956, from January 20 to May 20; his wife, Stella Dorsey, who was non-Indian, went along as his manager. By the March meeting, the Panel had in hand letters from Mrs. Dorsey, who wrote that he was well-received wherever he went: "Tom's appeal is to all levels and all ages, and reports from Calcutta, New Delhi and Madras have been glowing."

Because of the success of the first tour, Tom Two Arrows was sent again to Asia from November 1956 through February 1957. He performed in Japan, Korea, Taiwan, Cambodia, Vietnam, Thailand, Burma, and Malaya. An article in *The New York Herald Tribune*, dated 30 December 1956, gave some information on his tour:

Among the highlights of the Japanese tour was a visit with the Ainus, the aboriginal inhabitants of Japan. Mr. Tom Two Arrows had talks with two Ainu village chiefs and discovered that one of them was the proud possessor of a United States government pamphlet on Iroquois arts and crafts. They found close similarities among Iroquois and Ainu costume designs, homes of bark and thatch.... In Korea Mr. Two Arrows performed not only in Seoul but in other Korean cities and in the Republic of Korea Army and Air Force bases. Ten thousand soldiers attended one event and at the Dong Bang public theater nearby, 1,300 civilians jammed into the theater which seats only 900. In Japan, Korea and Formosa, Mr. Two Arrows has availed himself of every opportunity to discuss the dances, music and crafts of the Iroquois (and of the American Indian in general) with art leaders and simple villagers. In turn, the villagers—Ainus of Japan, Koreans, Formosans—demonstrated their ancient dances for the American visitor, while the professional dancers (of Korea) took special pleasure in engaging in technical discussions on the similarities and differences of American Indian and Oriental dance.

The article included statistics related to audiences: Tom Two Arrows's television performance in Japan reached an estimated two million viewers, and in Yokohama 12,000 people tried to buy tickets for the performance in an auditorium that had a 5,000 seat capacity.

The Dance Panel was always searching for additional Native American artists and groups. Even after they had chosen Tom Two Arrows, they continued to review other possibilities. At the September 1956 meeting, discussion centered on a group of performers headed by a man identified as Chief Rising Sun. "He was eighty-four years old, a spiritualist as well as an entertainer. Since the Panel didn't know about this group, they were requested to attend an audition at the Somerset Hotel on September 21st, and to report at the next Panel meeting." Either Chief Rising Sun changed his plans or the panelists couldn't attend the September show, for the October minutes record: "He has informed us that he will be giving a performance in Carnegie Hall on January 5, from 2:00 to 4:00 P.M., and hopes all the Panel members can attend. We will try to arrange for attendance at a public performance, but will notify the Chief that the Panel will not come to a special showing." Nothing ever came of this.

Another group mentioned at the September 1956 meeting were the "Hopitu" Dancers, an American Indian "opera" project. Apparently, this group had been rejected by the Music Panel, for the minutes state that "Miss Coleman saw this presentation and said it was not at all acceptable,

Tom Two Arrows performing before a village audience in Southeast Asia, 1956–1957. Dance Collection, The New York Public Library for the Performing Arts, Astor, Lenox, and Tilden Foundations

but when a definite plan is submitted, the Panel will look at the group." Again, there was no follow-up.

The Dance Panel returned several times to the idea of sending the Laubins, and specific discussions took place at the April 1957 meeting:

> Mr. Schnitzer said that the Laubins would need complete financing, but are ready to go at any time. They require a period of one month to prepare. Mr. Schnitzer mentioned the fact that it would be difficult even to organize the tour because to the Indians their dance is religion, not a performance. To preserve it as an art form it has fallen into the hands of white people like the Laubins...and two white performers alone would not be appropriate.

An interesting report about the Laubins surfaced at the June meeting. It had been reported to the State Department that a Native American group had appeared in Paris a few years earlier and that the French found them "most embarrassing." Walter Terry confirmed that this had been the Laubin group:

> Mr. Terry remarked that he had heard that the French had reacted unfavorably and believed it was because they had expected a Wild West show and were not prepared for a performance demonstrating Indian folklore. He also knew that during this tour the Laubins had used older tribal members, who, although they know and interpret the dances best, were not physically appealing to the French. In spite of all of this, Mr. Terry reiterated that of all Indian performing groups, the Laubins were the best, and suggested that in the selection of a group for the proposed current tour the Laubins could choose dancers for their physical attractiveness as well as for their dancing ability.

At that June 1957 meeting, the Dance Panel decided to approve the Laubin project and recommend to the State Department that they be sent on tour. The next time the minutes mention the Laubins was at the June 1961 meeting. They had not been sent abroad, and Walter Terry volunteered to talk with them again about preparing a show. He reiterated the fact that although they were white, "they have adapted the Indian way of life." Terry mentioned three Native Americans with whom the Laubins worked—Lizzie Yellowtail, Donald Deernose, and Tom He Does It.

At the September 1961 meeting the issue of the Laubins was raised again:

> There are constant requests for an American Indian team and Mr. Terry talked to the Laubins this summer. They would be willing to assemble a small company for the program, but they would have to have some guarantee that they would be sent. They do not need production money. They would need at least ten dancers to do ceremonials....Mr. Rosenfield felt this sounded ersatz; ten dancers cannot perform a ceremonial, and the fact that the Laubins are not Indian themselves might cause a problem. Mr.

Terry pointed out that they are more Indian than the Indians, and have dedicated their lives to these people.

The note in the minutes following this discussion is short but conclusive: "No decision was made at this meeting." As it turned out, the Laubins were never sent.

A presentation called *Dance of the Twelve Moons* was brought to the attention of the Panel at the 18 May 1961 meeting. "Arthur Junaluska of the American Indian Society of Creative Arts has presented this attraction recently, and will do so again. This is an American Indian troupe which could increase or decrease its personnel depending on the need of the Program."

Minutes of the June 1961 meeting include the report of a performance seen by panelist Lillian Moore earlier in the month: "Lillian Moore went to the presentation and regrets to say that the performances were much too amateurish to be considered by this Panel, although the material was fascinating. It reawakened her interest in the possibility of using American Indian material, if it were handled theatrically. The interest in the art of the American Indian is great in many areas of the world."

Gladys and Reginald Laubin. Dance Collection, The New York Public Library for the Performing Arts, Astor, Lenox, and Tilden Foundations.

Still trying to find a Native American group to send abroad, the Panel discussed a young man named Frank W. Joachimsthaler. "He is twenty-one years old, and he began the study of Indian lore ten years ago in the Boy Scouts. Since then he has danced in almost every western state, and has been on radio and television. He will be teaching Indian lore this summer in Muskegon, Michigan, and had his own television program in Montana." Joachimsthaler was a junior at the University of Montana and had decided "to devote his life to the study of the American Indian." He had danced for seven years with the Kahok Indian Dancers of Collinsville, Illinois, and had danced with the Flathead Indians as the only white performer. Panel members were interested in the letters and pictures he had sent; they decided to try to see his performances but nothing further was reported.

At the April 1962 meeting, Agnes de Mille brought to the attention of the Panel a scrapbook she had received containing material on a group of Boy Scouts from Wichita, Kansas. Calling themselves "Mi-Kam-Na-Mids of Wichita," they had made an extensive study of Native Americans. The minutes report: "They have not applied for a tour, but since there have been so many requests from the State Department for an American Indian troupe over the years, Miss de Mille thought the Panel might be interested in pursuing this further, even though the boys are not authentic Indians." Nothing further was done with this particular item of business. It seems possible that out of respect to de Mille everyone listened politely; however, a non-Indian Boy Scout troupe was not the answer.

In September 1962 there was brief discussion about a group called Stand Rock Indian Ceremonials. "Panel members who were familiar with the presentation seen each year at Wisconsin Dells, Wisconsin, did not believe it was authentic. If we send an Indian show, it will have to be better than this one." There seemed to be several groups drawing on Native American material, but their material was commercialized, poorly conceived and developed, and usually performed either by non-Indian or amateur groups.

The last discussion in 1962 about a Native American troupe took place at the October meeting. The Panel had received a letter from Dr. James O. Whittaker of Gustavus Adolphus College in St. Peter, Minnesota, "with a proposal to organize a group of American Indian dancers under the sponsorship of Arrow, Inc., an organization working on behalf of the American Indian." Whittaker wanted to work with the Executive Director of Arrow, Thomas Colosimo, and Congressman Ben Reifel, its Vice President.

The suggestion was to organize a group of performers consisting of approximately six smaller groups of twelve dancers each. The smaller groups would be chosen from various tribes throughout the country, each performing one or two of their unique tribal dances. Some dances would employ the entire group, and some individual performers could do specialty numbers.

Walter Terry said he knew about Arrow, Inc.; the Laubins used to belong to it but had withdrawn. He thought it was worth investigating Dr. Whittaker's suggestion about organizing a group of Native Americans. Emily Coleman wanted to find out if either the State Department or the Bureau of Indian Affairs could finance this endeavor. This was a rerun of the basic question that had affected previous discussions on Native American dance. No one was prepared to finance and organize the kind of groups that had been suggested over the years.

An overlapping preoccupation for the Dance Panel revolved around the issue of sending abroad some representation of American folk or square dance, or a combination of the two. This was first brought up at the September 1956 meeting when it was suggested that Ricky Holden, editor of a folk dance magazine and a well-known square dance caller, was anxious to form a company. It would consist of the best amateur folk dancers and be available for touring abroad. Panel members agreed to see him in action and to solicit opinions from experts in the field.

Holden gave a demonstration for the Music and Dance Panels the following January, and the response was that he was primarily oriented toward educational/recreational dance. At the March meeting Ann Barzel suggested various groups in Steamboat Springs, Colorado, and Kentucky. "Each group is specialized according to the dances in the specific area from which they come. If we could get them all together, a choice performance could be arranged. Lloyd Shaw, representing the Southwest, is a good showman, and works in a scholarly style." Barzel felt that young professional dancers could learn these steps easily "under the guidance of an expert such as Shaw for authenticity, and with a Broadway director for style and showmanship."

Walter Terry suggested that "ANTA write to Shaw to see if he would be willing to cooperate in such a venture." With no specific panelists credited with the ideas, the minutes record: "The Panel also felt that Bascom LaMar Lunsford should be contacted to represent the Southern folk dance styles in the same manner, and Ralph Paige the Northeastern. Thus all the different folk dance styles would be represented, with one overall theatrical person to hire the professional dancers and set the style for a show."

A motion was approved "to get a producer to investigate the possibility of preparing a show composed of regional folk dances from all over the United States, the choreography to be handled by the regional specialists named above." At their June meeting, the Dance Panel decided to approve this project and submit it to the State Department with a budget of between twenty and twenty-five thousand dollars. They felt that it was important to have a folk dance group, and none currently existed. It is hard to believe they expected the Department to fund it, given the complexity of the project and the small amount of money available. But hope springs eternal—and it certainly didn't hurt to ask!

Agnes de Mille was very interested in creating a company, which she tentatively called "American Lyric Theatre," based on material derived from folk dance. She submitted a one-page prospectus to the Dance Panel describing her plan:

> Our purpose here is to form a lyric theatre, drawing material and inspiration from American folklore, historic situations and themes, utilizing the services of our best composers, choreographers, writers and designers. The dance style will derive from our traditional inheritance—country and urban—the country dance, square dance, buck and wing, tap and jazz, the ballroom forms and the theatre heritage which can include ballet. In short, all devices and techniques which have endeared us to the world and for which we are internationally known. We will develop first the Anglo-Saxon and Negro forms and exclude the Indian....This company is designed to fill a gap in our national theatrical scene....It will fill the same place in the American dance that the Moiseyev troupe fills in the Russian. The company will approximate fifty singers and dancers....The composi-

tions will run from fifteen to thirty-five minutes and involve, on occasions, singing choruses and speech. The choreographers would include Michael Kidd, Robert Fosse, Gower Champion, John Butler, Herbert Ross, Jerome Robbins, Anna Sokolow, Katherine Dunham, Janet Collins, Danny Daniels, Buzz Miller, Hanya Holm, Gene Kelly, Agnes de Mille. The musicians would include Aaron Copland, Leonard Bernstein, Morton Gould, Trude Rittman, Lawrence Rosenthal, William Goldenberg, Hershy Kaye, and such classics as Stephen Foster, Gottschalk, Charles Ives and the popular melodists.

This ambitious plan went far beyond specific folk material offering the vision of an artistic entity that incorporated many sources and created original work. For the next two years de Mille struggled to raise money for her venture. In November 1960 she reported to the Panel that she had incorporated and formed a Board of Directors. She had also been in touch with the State Department, asking for financial assistance. They reiterated that there was no money for production costs, and she felt a sum of $300,000 was needed. De Mille also felt that "she had to establish the company on the American scene before it could be used for export."

In January 1961 de Mille reported to the Panel that she was finding it difficult to raise money: "Everyone thinks it is a superb idea but nobody gives money." She was now thinking about a company of twenty-four requiring $60,000–70,000 for one year; she would not embark on the project without $250,000 for three years. The minutes for the April 1962 meeting noted: "AGNES DE MILLE FOLK DANCE PROJECT: Miss de Mille is gathering money slowly for this project and will start working on it shortly. No foundation has offered support to date, although several attempts have been made." Neither the money nor the project materialized.

The Dance Panel never resolved the issue of creating a professional folk dance group, organizing experienced amateurs, or creating a company on the de Mille model that utilized folk dance as its base for new choreography. Instead, they chose to review an application that had come to them in 1960 from the Berea College (Kentucky) Folk Dance Group. The first discussion about the group had taken place at the November meeting: "Miss Barzel stated that they have a fine folk dance group which presents programs with great success in their part of the country. They do beautiful work, running sets, accompaniments to 17th century ballads, etc."

The application from the Berea folk dancers raised the question about sending college groups. There had already been applications from several schools, such as Smith College, Ohio State University, Gallaudet College, Bennington College, and the Juilliard School of Music. Panelist George Beiswanger was asked to set up an ad hoc committee to make recommendations about fitting academic groups into the program and to establish a list of outstanding groups.[1] Martha Hill, Agnes de Mille, and William

Bales were proposed as members; Martha Hill suggested they should go to Kentucky to look at the Berea folk dancers and report back on their artistic merits.

George Beiswanger prepared a report from the subcommittee on academic projects and distributed it at the March 1961 meeting. He had been in contact with the President of Berea College and had received photographs and additional information about their performance dates. Ann Barzel said that she would see one of their three Illinois performances, and de Mille was advised that there would be an April show at Berea.

After looking at the photographs, Martha Hill noted that the costumes represented only English dances. Barzel remarked that the Berea dancers were "definitely of English descent and tradition, and this is what they specialize in." Both Beiswanger and Bales questioned the theatricality of the Berea dancers, and Bales suggested what he called a "junior Agnes de Mille company." By this he meant putting together a program of choreographed dances based on folk themes; Sophie Maslow's *Folksay*, Doris Humphrey's *Shakers*, and Donald McKayle's *Games* were mentioned as examples.[2] If someone were hired to organize this, there could be a joint program with the Berea dancers. Since this issue always arose in regard to folk dance presentations, the panelists decided to wait until they had seen the Berea dancers before exploring other directions.

Ann Barzel reported at the May 1961 meeting that she had seen the Berea folk dancers perform several times in the Chicago area. "They were charming, wholesome and sweet, and would be good for the American specialists program abroad. It is not a theatrical program, but they have graduates all over the world, and can work with the international students. It was pointed out that the American Specialists Branch does not use groups, but individuals. Therefore this project would have to be considered for the President's Program."

The Berea dancers generally invited audience participation after their performance: "The question was discussed as to whether the Asians would like an audience participation show, or whether they would be too shy and unused to it to join in." Panelist Hyman Faine suggested this kind of format would work in South America, as the cultural barriers were not as great.

The Dance Panel could have turned down the Berea dancers, particularly since their repertory was somewhat limited and only represented one part of the American folk heritage. In spite of much hesitation, however, they were approved and sent on a three-month tour in the summer of 1962 to Mexico, El Salvador, Guatemala, Honduras, Nicaragua, Costa Rica, Panama, Colombia, and Ecuador. Performances took place in thirty cities, with thirty-eight live concerts and several nationwide television shows.

The reports on the Berea dancers were all positive. The first was a cable to the State Department in June 1962 after the opening performance in Monterrey, Mexico. "3500 students and middle class spontaneously

IGA

Instituto Guatemalteco Americano

Grupo folklórico de Berea College

Actividades de Junio

8a. Av. 9-12, Zona 1   Tel. 25438

ABOVE: *Members of the Berea College Folk Dance Group on tour in Latin America, 1962. Courtesy of Berea College.*

LEFT: *Announcement of the Berea College Folk Dance Group's appearance at the Guatemalan-American Institute, June 1962. Courtesy of Berea College.*

applaud Berea throughout opening performance. Dancers effectiveness exceeds expectations." A longer report came in September after the tour had ended:

> There were sixteen dancers and four musicians. The artistic quality of the Berea dancers does not, of course, measure up to the highest professional standards since these are young non-professionals. However, as students they made a fine impression and were successful in their objective of giving the average Latin American student an opportunity to meet with our students, and participate in our folk culture.

The Berea dancers performed in theaters and in nontheatrical settings such as gymnasiums, patios, and cafeterias, and they usually invited the audience to participate at the end of performances. The advance publicity "clearly stated that the dancers were from a college, and they were never judged by professional standards or in a professional atmosphere." Eighty-five percent of the audience was middle-class or made up of high school or university students. Admission was charged to only five of the thirty-eight performances. "In Colombia a group of folk dancers from the Bolshoi Ballet were present at the same time as Berea, and whereas they were technically perfect, they charged high admission prices. Because Berea was free, they had an audience of 20,000 as compared to 1,000 for the Russian troupe."

The final word came from Robert F. Jordan, Cultural Affairs Officer of the American Embassy in Honduras:

> The presentation of the Berea College Folk Dancers in Tegucigalpa is considered one of the highlights of the Cultural Exchange Program. Not only did the dancers perform splendidly but they also were equally effective onstage with their pleasant personalities, interest in meeting Honduran students, and their desire to learn about Honduran folklore dances and songs. The fact that many of the Berea students were not reticent about using their somewhat limited knowledge of Spanish certainly added to the good impression.... A fine program of precise dancing was topped off, to the intense delight of all those present, when the Berea students went down into the audience and selected Honduran partners for an old-fashioned square dance.... During the day Berea College dancers...met with Honduran folklore groups for an interchange of dance and music.

While the Dance Panel had been in agreement about sending abroad folk dance groups, over a period of four years they argued about sending a popular dance revue. At the very first Panel meeting in October 1954 the minutes record: "It was felt that it might be very interesting because of its popularity with the American masses but that type of art might be considered unwise or vulgar to the type of people we were trying most to impress." Some of the panelists had suggestions about revues encompassing ragtime, swing, Charleston, jitterbug, and the Lindy Hop, all of which would also include singers and narration.

The minutes of the February 1955 meeting record Walter Terry's suggestion for a "package" show that would include popular songs and jazz.
"This would draw a large audience and Mr. Terry specifically had it in
mind for South America. The popular American song hits that would be
featured are sold by European distributors of the record companies and
therefore would be familiar to foreign audiences."

After the February meeting, Terry approached choreographer Rod
Alexander about creating "a survey from ragtime and jazz and swing to
current song and dance trends." Alexander had a broad dance background
and had worked successfully as a choreographer for movies, Broadway,
night clubs, as well as the new television variety shows. He had studied
ballet, modern, and jazz dance with Jack Cole, Hanya Holm, Carmelita
Maracci, Lester Horton, Tatiana Riabouchinska, Elizabeth Anderson-
Ivantzova, Nick Castle, and Edna McRae.

During the 1940s Alexander had worked with Jack Cole at Columbia
Pictures (1945–1948), then did a nightclub tour with the Jack Cole
Dancers (1948–1949). He first danced on Broadway in *Inside U.S.A.*
(1948), a musical choreographed by Helen Tamiris in which he was
teamed with Valerie Bettis. He then partnered Bambi Linn in Tamiris's
Great to be Alive (1952), and they continued to dance as a team both in
night clubs and on television. The two appeared on the television special
Your Show of Shows (1953), for which they also staged the dances, and
later on *Max Liebman Presents*. Alexander choreographed the film version of *Carousel* in 1956 and in 1957 staged the dances for *The Best
Things in Life Are Free*; in 1958 he choreographed *Shinbone Alley* for
Broadway and later the dances for the show *Thirteen Daughters*.[3]

Rod Alexander's plans were presented to the Panel at the April 1955
meeting. They included his dance partner Bambi Linn, who was also his
wife. Linn had studied with Mikhail Mordkin and Hanya Holm. The
original Aggie in *Oklahoma!* (1943), she had created the role of Louise in
Carousel (1945). Later she appeared as a guest soloist with American Ballet Theatre and in the Broadway show *I Can Get It For You Wholesale*
(1962).

Linn and Alexander envisioned, aside from themselves, a cast of "four
singers who could dance and four dancers who could sing, a pianist and a
drummer." Their program was designed for a South American tour as "a
cavalcade of America in dance from 1850 to the present." The panelists
had various suggestions. Lucia Chase wanted the finale to be on a positive
note. Emily Coleman wanted "narration and commentary in the language
of the country where they would be playing." Walter Terry wanted the
Spanish and Portuguese translations to be prepared in this country in
advance, so that our viewpoint, rather than a local one, would be
expressed. Edward Mangum, who had completed a tour of Asia for
ANTA investigating facilities, bookings, and other matters, noted that
"99% of the Asians would be completely in the dark upon seeing this. It
would take an hour to explain the incidents depicted, as these isolated

instances of history are not typical of America as the Asians know it."

Discussion continued regarding financing such a project, and the suggestion was made that, in order to cover production costs, Alexander do this first as a television special. The panelists wanted Alexander to submit a budget showing his expected deficit. Walter Terry suggested that perhaps the Music Panel should be consulted regarding the selection of musicians and singers. Ultimately, Alexander was encouraged to go ahead with his plans.

It took two years to complete the project, which was finally ready in 1958. Called *Dance Jubilee*, the show toured the United States that year under the auspices of Columbia Concerts. The Dance Panel's review was largely favorable, and the show was sent abroad from October 1959 to March 1960. The five-month tour went to Greece, Lebanon, Iran, Afghanistan, Pakistan, India, Burma, Thailand, Cambodia, Malaya, Singapore, Hong Kong, Taiwan, Korea, Okinawa, and the Philippines. *Dance Jubilee* was the only attraction of its kind sponsored by the Dance Panel.

By the time *Dance Jubilee* was ready to tour, Bambi Linn and Rod Alexander had split up, both as a dance team and as marriage partners. Gemze de Lappe took Linn's place as Alexander's lead female dancer. She had been in many musicals—*Miss Liberty* (1949), which Jerome Robbins had choreographed, *Oklahoma!*, *Paint Your Wagon* (1951), and, later, the New York City Center revival of *Brigadoon* (1962)—all with choreography by Agnes de Mille. She had also played a leading role in de Mille's *The Harvest According* for Ballet Theatre in 1952. In the *Dance Jubilee* tour Rod

IN CALCUTTA

PRESIDENT EISENHOWER'S CULTURAL PROGRAMME PRESENTS

ROD ALEXANDER'S

a panorama of american popular dance & song **dance Jubilee**

CALYPSO CARNAVAL, November 21
Sponsored by
The Calypso Carnaval Committee
AT THE
Great Eastern Hotel, Main Ballroom
NOVEMBER 22 EVENING
New Empire
NOVEMBER 23 AND 24 AT 6 P.M.
Sponsored by
The Indo-American Society
All performances in aid of the Governor's After-Care TB Fund

Program for Rod Alexander's Dance Jubilee, *Calcutta, 1959. Private collection, New York.*

Alexander and de Lappe were given equal billing as stars. Two dancers, Carmen Gutierrez and Lou Kristofer, were featured as well as the singer Dale Monroe. The others were listed as a group—Audre Deckman, Carole D'Andrea, Bella Sholom, Wakefield Poole, Patrick Cummings, and Patrick Helm. The musical director was Daniel Gordon (pianist-conductor), and the musicians were John Carisi (trumpet), Morton Lewis (saxophone), Steve Perlow (saxophone), and Calvin Santo (drummer).[4]

The show opened with a number called "Overture: George M. Cohan Medley." This was followed by "Minstrel Dances: circa 1880, Stephen Foster Medley, Rhythm in Precision, The Strut, The Cakewalk." According to the program note,

> The Minstrel Show had its origin in American Negro song and dance, and became extremely popular in the last decades of the nineteenth century, not only in America but in Europe also. Stephen Foster, first great American composer and writer of our well-beloved popular songs, wrote some of his most famous songs for minstrel shows. The strut, the cakewalk and the rhythm dance are the same as those performed on the streets of villages and rural communities in the South. Though simple in construction, they were infused with an intricate syncopation and unusual style by the Negro people who created them.

The next section was "Spiritual Songs," followed by "City Dances: Strolling through the Park, The Waltz." "The people in the cities of the northern areas of the United States favored elegant and dignified dances, mostly European in origin, spiced with humor and flirtation as in the schottische and polka, or garnished with sentiment like the waltz."

After this came the song "Toyland," followed by "Theatre Dances: circa 1900, The Toyshop, and Puppet Dance Pierrot and Pierrette." The commentary emphasized the importance of turn-of-the-century operetta; Victor Herbert's name was given as the foremost composer of this form. Next came "Folk Dance Suite: Black is the Color of My True Love's Hair, Quartet, The Wayfaring Stranger, Gently Johnny, The Hoedown." The accompanying text read:

> The pioneers who settled the valleys and mountain areas of the vast American frontiers were forced to create their own musical entertainment. With the aid of a fiddle or a guitar, they made up songs about their work, their loves or their religion, and often danced as they sang these ballads. When they were in a mood for celebration they invariably danced the square dance of "Hoedown."

"Alexander's Ragtime Band" came after intermission, then a suite of ballroom dances—the Turkey Trot, Castle Walk, and Maxixe—along with the following explanation: "Ragtime was a form of jazz which caught the fancy of the entire American nation in 1910. A new ballroom craze was started. The 'one-step,' the 'two-step,' the 'bunny hug,' and the 'turkey trot' were the rage of the day. The Castle Walk and the Castle Maxixe were popularized by Vernon and Irene Castle, a famous dance team."

Without having seen Rod Alexander's show it is hard to estimate its length. There were seven more numbers: "Jazz Craze: circa 1920 (Songs of the 20's, The Raccoon, The Collegiate, The Vamp, Vo-do-di-o, The Blackbottom)," "The Blues: circa 1929," "Movie Dances: circa 1935 (Top

Hat, The Continental)," "Restless Lover," "Theatre Dances: circa 1940 (Law of the West: A Story Ballet)," "Song Hit of 1950," and "Finale: I Got Rhythm."

According to the program, "Jazz had made considerable progress by 1920, and the new dances which were created had a new syncopated beat, a fresh vitality and more freedom than those of the previous decade." The note for blues was short: "The blues is a further progression of Jazz music, and like its forerunner, the spiritual, creates a mood of loneliness." A note in the movie dance section explained swing: "Swing music was used as an accompaniment for dances in movies in 1930.[5] Rhythm, style and sophistication were the characteristics of this form of American dance." The note for the "Finale" was interesting: "The dances of the present day vary greatly in style and tempo, and the finale brings the style of dancing up to date, closing with the Lindy Hop, which many consider the national folk dance of America."

The fairly extensive text was handled by a narrator hired for different cities and countries, meaning that audiences could understand everything that was said. Wherever the show was presented, its government sponsorship was acknowledged. The program credits mentioned "President Eisenhower's Special International Program for Cultural Presentations" and also thanked ANTA for suggesting the creation of *Dance Jubilee*.

Dance Jubilee presented a watered-down, commercialized version of America's song and dance traditions, one that was familiar from television and Broadway. There was no mention in any of the narration, and no representation in any of the numbers, of African-Americans or African-American influence on minstrel shows, jazz, blues, and popular dances such as the Turkey Trot, Blackbottom, and Lindy Hop. Today we would send abroad a very different *Dance Jubilee*.[6]

The Kennedy Center for the Performing Arts sits securely on the banks of the Potomac—a landmark in our nation's capital. Inside its grand facade a bustle of intense activity continues from morning to midnight. Visitors from all over the world tour its five theaters, gift shops, and grand foyers. People of all ages attend formal and informal performances, and a wide range of music, dance, and theater is available on a year-round basis.

Today, we take the Kennedy Center for granted, but it took many years for Congress to be convinced that Americans needed a national cultural center. In September 1958, when the 85th Congress passed Public Law 85–874, "provid[ing] for a National Cultural Center which will be constructed with funds raised by voluntary contributions, on a site made available in the District of Columbia," a major victory was won for domestic support of the arts. After President Kennedy was killed, this center was renamed the John F. Kennedy Center for the Performing Arts.

There is a direct correlation between the international exchange program initiated by Eisenhower in 1954 and the domestic arts support enacted into law only four years later. Companion measures to provide for the erection of a National Cultural Center were first introduced in the Senate in February 1958 by Senator J. William Fulbright, Democrat from Arkansas, and in the House by Representative Frank Thompson, Jr., Democrat from New Jersey. The original wording made it very clear that this center represented a continuation of the idea of the arts as a diplomatic tool:

> This Act is intended to strengthen the ties which unite the United States with other nations and to assist in the further growth and development of friendly, sympathetic, and peaceful relations between the United States and the other nations of the world by demonstrating the cultural interests and achievements of the people of the United States. This is particularly necessary at this time when the Soviet Union and other totalitarian nations are spending vast sums for the arts in an attempt to lead the peoples of the world to believe that those countries produce civilization's best efforts in the fine arts. It is demonstrably true that wars begin in the minds of men and that it is in the minds of men that the defenses of peace must be constructed.[1]

Testifying in April 1958 before the Senate's Committee on Public Works and the Subcommittee on Public Buildings and Grounds, Senator

Fulbright made a direct connection between the arts and foreign relations. In his extensive testimony, he emphasized his conviction, as a longtime member of the Committee on Foreign Relations, that we had created an extremely negative impression abroad because Washington was the only national capital without a center for the performing arts.

In support of his argument, Fulbright cited the recent international Tchaikovsky competition held in Moscow, and the fact that a twenty-three-year-old American pianist, Van Cliburn, had won the $6,250 first prize. The reaction in Moscow to Cliburn was double-edged; the Russians loved his virtuosity but were appalled that he was virtually unknown in America. The same was true of another American competitor, Daniel Pollack, who had won ninth place.

Fulbright made a strong plea for America's support of the performing arts both overseas and at home:

> The great virtue of the performing arts is that they do transcend the barriers of language. When Mr. Van Cliburn went to Moscow, of course, he didn't need to speak Russian to make an impression. I recently read a story that the New York City Ballet was in Tokyo and received an unprecedented ovation from the Japanese. When you consider what difficulty our diplomats and politicians have in communicating with the Russians, this ought to be very impressive; at least our musicians can gain a favorable response from these people; and this is not only with regard to our antagonists, that is, the Russians, but this is particularly important with regard to the uncommitted countries, countries like India, Burma, Indonesia, and any of the countries in Latin America, who are now trying to evaluate as best they can the relative merits of this country, the western civilization, and the Russians.... In recent hearings before the Committee on Foreign Relations, I have taken occasion to ask nearly every important witness—many of them experts in the fields of political relations...if they think it is significant that the Russians do promote so successfully the arts.... And everyone of them invariably replies that they think it is very significant.[2]

The proposed cultural center was to be situated on the Mall opposite the National Gallery of Art. However, controversy arose because of a bill proposed by Senator Clinton P. Anderson, Democrat from New Mexico, who wanted to build a National Air Museum on the same site. With Senator Anderson, Representative Thompson, and cooperative Federal agencies, Senator Fulbright worked out a compromise that eventually located the proposed center at its current site, on the Potomac River in the Foggy Bottom area of Washington, D.C.

The Senate passed the bill establishing the National Cultural Center on June 20. The House of Representatives was less receptive. A major stumbling block was the Subcommittee on Buildings and Grounds of the Committee on Public Works. When it met on August 5, supporters of the center mustered all their forces to get the bill through the House. Among the documents supporting their position was a letter from President Eisenhower addressed to Representative Charles A. Buckley, Democrat from New York and Chairman of the Committee on Public Works. It read in part:

> I am writing you with reference to legislation now pending before your committee which would authorize the establishment of a national cultural center here in Washington on a site made available by the Federal Government with funds raised by voluntary contributions. There has long been a need for more adequate facilities in the Nation's Capital for the presentation of the performing arts. An auditorium and other facilities such as are provided by the pending legislation, established and supported by contributions from the public, would be a center of which the entire Nation could be proud. I hope that the Congress will complete action on this legislation during this session.

When Representative Frank Thompson was called to testify, he emphasized that the legislation had been introduced on a bipartisan basis. He also reviewed the history of attempts to create a major cultural center in the nation's capital. He pointed out that George Washington during his presidency had commissioned Major Pierre L'Enfant "to plan the Federal City as a cultural and civic center of the new United States. Indeed, the Founding Fathers saw the Nation's Capital as a new Athens, a city of light and learning." Congressional proposals in 1913 and 1937 to establish a national cultural center had failed. In 1955 Thompson himself proposed the creation of a commission to plan such a center; although it received support from several congressmen, it too had failed.

There were frequent references to the international exchange program during the House Subcommittee hearings. Representative Thompson's remarks included information about a tour sponsored by the program:

> *The Wall Street Journal,* in a front-page story on May 15, 1958, declared that while Vice President Nixon and his entourage were running into angry mobs, the New York Philharmonic Symphony on its South American tour at the same time was everywhere greeted with warmth and affection by cheering fans. And on May 10, 1958, *The New York World Telegram* said editorially that—"There is a faintly encouraging counterpoint to last week's savage outburst in Caracas—one which this Nation might well nurture and exploit. New York's Philharmonic Symphony, currently on tour in Latin America, has been the object of adulation at almost every stop. In Caracas, particularly, mobs were as wild in their enthusiasm for conductor Leonard Bernstein as they were in their disenchantment with Vice President Nixon a few days later. The Philharmonic's success under State Department-ANTA sponsorship duplicates triumphant cultural forays into ninety-odd countries by 100 other groups of American artists since the program's inception. Cultural successes do not, of course, compensate for this country's economic and political failures in

Latin America and elsewhere. But they have proved their value in helping to win the minds of alien and suspicious people. The gentlefolk in the Kremlin delight in picturing Americans as Babbitts braying in a cultural desert. Tours such as the Philharmonic's provide a sure and relatively inexpensive way of proving them wrong.

The New York Philharmonic tour, which had taken place the previous spring, was a vivid reminder of the success of the international exchange program and a testimonial to the validity and importance of the arts. After visiting Caracas, Venezuela, the orchestra played to enthusiastic audiences in Colombia, Ecuador, Peru, Bolivia, Paraguay, Chile, Argentina, Uruguay, Brazil, and Mexico.

The House Public Works Committee invited Senator Alexander Wiley, Republican from Wisconsin, to testify on behalf of the National Cultural Center; his testimony made a point of connecting the arts with foreign policy: "The Nation does need this National Cultural Center. America needs it for enjoyment by our own citizens. America needs it as a beacon to the free world. . . . I say this as a senior member of the Foreign Relations Committee." His thoughts were echoed in a statement by Representative Frances P. Bolton, Republican from Ohio, who stated that "my work on the Foreign Affairs Committee has brought me an increased realization of the importance of the arts in our foreign relations, and of the use other countries make of these in their foreign relations."

Representative James Wright, Democrat from Texas, had not been known for his interest in the arts, but he too was quite articulate about his support of the project: "I want to commend our colleague, Mr. Thompson, for his display of vision in championing this legislation. When I think of Mr. Thompson I think of the statement of Solomon, when he said, 'Where there is no vision the people perish.'"

Wright commented that the cultural center would be important in the conduct of international affairs. "People come here from the capitals of Europe and ask where the opera house is, and we have to hang our heads a little bit when we say we don't have one." Wright felt that in the past he and many others had found it easy to be skeptical of people's interest in culture, but the time had come to realize its importance. He was convinced that the American people and his own constituents would support the legislation:

> I haven't the least question in my mind but that the American people will contribute generously to the erection of this Cultural Center. I support this conclusion by something that happened this year, at Fort Worth. Fort Worth is a cow town. It has not exactly been noted as a cultural center. And not all of us have money, but we erected a Casa Manana down there this year for the performance of theatrical arts. A lot of people said, "This thing will be a drag on the municipality. Nobody will back this Casa Manana. People will not pay money to see theatricals and light operas in Fort Worth." In the first two months of operation they have yielded a $10,000 profit each month on operations.

Money was an important issue in the August hearings. The Fulbright-Thompson bill passed by the Senate in June had stipulated that the Center would be built on ten acres. The Federal Government owned nine acres and would have to purchase the additional acre from private owners. In a lengthy statement at the House Subcommittee hearings in August, Representative James G. Fulton of Pennsylvania spoke of the importance of the arts in international affairs and in daily life in America. As an example, he named Pittsburgh as a city where—with community support—tax money was being spent to build a new civic auditorium. The community was committed to raising whatever funds were necessary in order to create the best structure possible.

Fulton also connected the proposed center to international exchange. He asked permission to put in the record a statement to the committee by Robert W. Dowling, the chairman of the ANTA board and an active participant from the beginning of Eisenhower's Emergency Fund.[3] Dowling was on a business trip out of the country and therefore did not appear in person. In his statement, he affirmed his belief that any money needed for the National Cultural Center could be raised. He pointed out that he had presented plans to President Truman in 1951 for such a center, and had served as Vice Chairman of the District of Columbia Auditorium Commission during President Eisenhower's first administration. In the report submitted by this group, the Foggy Bottom area near the Potomac was recommended for the center.

Dowling made explicit reference to the exchange program: "When we send abroad an exchange program, exchange is a misnomer if we can't receive something here in return. These have been making friends for our country. But then artists, producers, musicians ask when they can come here." Dowling did not want the building to include a convention hall as it should be kept to the "field of culture and artistic achievement." He stressed the availability of parking, for he wanted it to be "a theater of the people."

The Fulbright-Thompson bill finally made it through the House of Representatives. When Eisenhower signed the bill into law in September 1958, it was a sign that the recognition of our arts abroad had raised their visibility and support at home. The repeated mention in the Senate and House hearings of the link between foreign affairs and the arts had elicited enthusiasm and support from many who had previously been either negative or neutral.

This is not to say that all the project's enemies had disappeared; it was simply that their number had diminished in the face of testimony about the success of American orchestras, ballet companies, and theater groups abroad. Gary O. Larson summed up the change in *The Reluctant Patron*: "No longer a political liability or the special interest of northeastern liberals, arts advocacy in Congress began to emerge as another weapon in the politician's arsenal of popular causes."[4]

Robert Dowling was a strong voice in 1958 for the establishment of the National Cultural Center; he spoke as someone with several years' experience in helping to start and manage ANTA's work with the USIA and State Department. Another connection with ANTA and Eisenhower's Emergency Fund was Roger Stevens. Stevens had served on ANTA's international exchange committee since 1954, when the very first contract with the State Department was signed. He continued to serve on the committee until 1960, when he was also the ANTA treasurer and a member of the board. In 1961 Stevens was appointed chairman of the board of trustees of the National Cultural Center. His mandate was to begin laying the groundwork to make the 1958 legislation a reality, and to help raise funds for development and construction.[5]

That was just the beginning of Stevens's involvement in government and the arts. In early 1964, shortly after President Kennedy's death, President Lyndon B. Johnson appointed a committee to develop a policy for the arts during his administration. This group consisted of Assistant Secretary of State Lucius D. Battle, violinist Isaac Stern, lawyer Abe Fortas, and White House Press Secretary Pierre Salinger. Their suggestions included improving existing federal programs in the arts, increasing private sector support, and planning programming and development of the Kennedy Center as a national arts showcase. This committee also recommended that the position of special arts consultant to the president be continued. Under Kennedy, August Heckscher had served in this capacity, and the recommendation was that Roger Stevens succeed Heckscher.[6] Another recommendation was that a nine-member Presidential Board on the Arts should be created, with advisory panels in the various arts.

In May 1964 Stevens was appointed special assistant for the arts to President Johnson. In February 1965 Johnson appointed Stevens chairman of the National Council on the Arts, which had been authorized by Congress only six months earlier as a Presidential advisory group consisting of prominent arts figures. At the same time, Johnson named the members of the newly created Council. Stevens thus played a major role in identifying individuals who would be part of this important new advisory group. One of his choices was Agnes de Mille, who had served for many years on ANTA's Dance Panel.[7]

Shortly after the act establishing the National Foundation on the Arts and Humanities was signed on 29 September 1965, Stevens was appointed the first head of the National Endowment for the Arts (NEA). For many arts advocates the creation of the NEA was the culmination of years of struggle.[8] The existence of NEA ensured that the arts were an official part of the national landscape; it also meant that taxpayers' dollars could be used for projects at home. From the very beginning, the funding of NEA projects was based on shared public-private initiatives, premised on the idea of free enterprise and government involvement.

As first head of the NEA, Roger Stevens brought years of experience from ANTA, especially in issues related to government and the arts. As a member of ANTA's international committee and its board, he knew the difficulties involved in partnerships with the private sector, even if commercial bookings supplemented income and extended tours.

Stevens was well aware that the ANTA staff and panels were constantly making choices that would reflect on the American government. The word censorship never shows up in panel minutes or reports, but congressional hearings reflect an attitude that control of content and personnel would not be remiss in a government supported program. Attempts to influence panel decisions were not unknown, either from powerful private individuals or from congressmen eager to promote their own constituents.

The essential nature of how to use government funding was always a question; whether money should go to entertainment for a mass audience or to artists of more complex work intended for an elite audience. Stevens understood the importance of the innovative panel system that ANTA had developed. He was well aware of the value of decisions made by a panel of professional peers, whose discussions and choices could reflect years of experience. He also knew that panels had to consist of different kinds of professionals in a particular field and that geographic diversity was important. Stevens brought a wealth of knowledge and history to his job as head of the NEA; he knew the players and the issues.

It was through the international exchange program of the 1950s that Stevens, Dowling, and others gained the administrative experience and refined their ideas about the arts and public policy. Thus, in January 1963, the State Department's decision to terminate its contract with ANTA and take over the administration of the performing arts exchange program itself signaled the end of an era. For almost ten years the ANTA board, assisted by a wide variety of professionals in the arts, shared monthly meetings and wide-ranging conversations.

The decision to shift the program from ANTA to the State Department was met with dismay by ANTA and the members of the various panels. In October 1962 the State Department commissioned a report issued the following December surveying the entire "cultural presentations program," as it was called. The authors were Roy E. Larsen, chairman of the Executive Committee of Time, Inc., and Glenn G. Wolfe, Foreign Service Officer.[9]

The report was quite firm in stating that ANTA should no longer help administer the exchange programs, a conclusion, predictably, that troubled ANTA and the members of its panels, who awaited the opportunity to raise questions. The result was a joint meeting on 17 January 1963 between the International Cultural Exchange Service (ICES) of ANTA, members of the State Department, and several dozen individuals then serving on the various panels. Altogether there were forty-eight people present at the meeting, which lasted three hours.

The meeting was chaired by Mrs. Alwyn Inness-Brown, who had served as chair of ICES for many years. The spokesman for the State Department was Lucius D. Battle, Assistant Secretary of State for Education and Cultural Affairs.[10] The discussion centered on the 1962 Larsen-

Wolfe report praising the international exchange program for its domestic as well as foreign impact.

It was very important, noted the authors, to recognize the domestic impact of the program. Because of the program, American artists had gained both a modicum of stability and national visibility. The authors also emphasized that the United States as a whole had gained prestige all over the world as a result of its performing arts exports.

After praising the program, the authors expressed concern that neither ANTA nor the panels, because of their isolation from foreign policy issues, could adequately do long-range planning. The State Department, they felt, was in a better position to decide where and when to send artists. The authors praised the panels for emphasizing serious art and felt this emphasis should continue; they also asserted that the program's long-range goals could best be served by targeting audiences consisting of leaders in all fields. It was also suggested that more of the budget should be allocated to youth and college groups who could reach out to similar constituencies abroad.

While acknowledging that the international exchange program was not receiving the recognition it deserved, Larsen and Wolfe asserted that this was partly due to its divided administrative organization. Housing the program in Washington, literally as well as figuratively, seemed to them a more viable way of consolidating efforts and even allaying Congressional doubts about its validity. The Larsen-Wolfe report recommended that an arts advisory group oversee all activities of the international exchange program, be involved in policy discussions, and provide assistance to the State Department.

At the joint meeting, there was deep concern expressed by ANTA and the various panel members that the new structure would create excessive government control over policy. They could not understand how the program could be based in Washington—which in 1963 could easily seem a very provincial town—or picture the State Department dealing with artists' temperaments and schedules. New York was the center of the arts, and most of the professionals involved with the program since 1954 were active there on a daily basis. The State Department, however, had no qualms about basing the program in Washington or dealing with artistic temperament. Lucius D. Battle spoke on behalf of the State Department: "Let me say that the cultural presentations program has no monopoly on temperament. You have temperament in terms of the Congressional groups and V.I.P.'s that go around, and all sorts of lecturers that go out, so temperament we know about."

The Dance Panel's Hyman Faine wanted to focus less on particulars and more on the basic issue. "This program has been looked at by many as a prototype of the whole relationship between the federal government and the performing arts." He compared eliminating the contract with ANTA to building a bomber or conducting explorations of outer space. "Aren't there areas in which the government feels that while it has the primary responsibility, the nature of the project itself calls for it to be left to knowledgeable people in the field?"

The three-hour meeting resulted in much discussion, but the ANTA contract was still canceled. However, when the NEA was created in 1965, it was indeed a separate agency, headed by professionals as administrators and heavily dependent upon panels for recommendations.

The ties between cultural and foreign diplomacy is a very real issue that still exists. Eisenhower's Emergency Program was conceived as a weapon in the Cold War to make the United States more competitive with the Soviet Union and to persuade undecided or left-leaning countries that the American way of life was superior to Soviet communism. The question both then and now about the relationship between politics and art was: are they strange bedfellows or compatible roommates?

The artists who went abroad in the 1950s and 1960s were armed not with propaganda messages, but with the spiritual power that infused their art. They communicated above all through their concern with sound, image, shape, and energy, conveying a personal vision that derived from their imagination, heritage, and training. It was this vision that was so powerful. It was not their intent to talk or preach about the greatness of America. The excellence of what they did showed the world that the United States was not a country interested only in weapons, refrigerators, and movies.

Today, we do not need a Cold War to support the arts either at home or abroad. The arts have their own value and, fortunately, the operation of Eisenhower's Emergency Fund from the very beginning reinforced this. Conceptually and practically, the panel system was brilliant; it ensured professional standards of assessment and minimized government control and censorship. The Dance Panel minutes constantly reinforce the importance of the international exchange program not only for survival of the various companies, but also as a significant factor in their recognition on home territory.

Sadly, the press and the public did not take the program to heart; indeed they were often in the dark about what it was doing. Its domestic impact was unmistakable however, on the members of Congress; these were the people who learned of the program's success in hearings and through personal contacts.

The performing arts today have the same diplomatic power that they had in 1954. When American performing artists first went abroad it was as an experiment in international relations and foreign policy. They succeeded, not because they were a weapon in the Cold War, but because they had something to say to people everywhere.

Notes

Introduction

1. Robert H. Haddow, *Pavilions of Plenty: Exhibiting American Culture Abroad in the 1950s* (Washington: Smithsonian Institution Press, 1997); Reinhold Wagnleitner, *Coca-Colaization and the Cold War: The Cultural Mission of the United States in Austria after the Second World War* (Chapel Hill: University of North Carolina Press, 1994); Elizabeth A. Fones-Wolf, *Selling Free Enterprise: The Business Assault on Labor and Liberalism 1945–1960* (Urbana: University of Illinois Press, 1994).
2. Michael Kammen, "Culture and the State in America," *Journal of American History*, 83, no. 3 (Dec. 1996), p. 801.
3. Henry R. Luce, *The American Century* (New York: Farrar and Rinehart, 1941), pp. 22–37.
4. Serge Guibault, *How New York Stole the Idea of Modern Art: Abstract Expressionism, Freedom, and the Cold War,* trans. Arthur Goldhammer (Chicago: University of Chicago Press, 1983); Jane DeHart Mathews, "Art and Politics in Cold War America," *American Historical Review*, 81, no. 4 (Oct. 1976), pp. 762–787.
5. Penny Von Eschen, *Race Against Empire: Black Americans and Anticolonialism 1937–1957* (Ithaca, N.Y.: Cornell University Press, 1997), pp. 122–124.

Prologue

1. Nicolas Nabokov, *Bagázh: Memoirs of a Russian Cosmopolitan* (New York: Atheneum, 1975), p. 243. For a description of the festival, see Peter Coleman, *The Liberal Conspiracy: The Congress for Cultural Freedom and the Struggle for the Mind of Postwar Europe* (London: Macmillan, 1989), pp. 45–57.
2. Eva Cockcroft, "Abstract Expressionism: Weapon of the Cold War," *Artforum*, 12 (June 1974), pp. 39–41; Guilbaut, *How New York Stole the Idea of Modern Art.*

Eisenhower's Fund

1. The Bureau of Educational and Historical and Cultural Affairs Historical Collection, Special Collections Division, University of Arkansas Libraries, Fayetteville. As a great deal of primary material comes from this source, notes will only be used when the reference is from other libraries and archives. When material from this collection does requires an endnote, the acronym ABECA will be used. The collection was recently reorganized, and a finding aid created. Material can be located by identifying the broad category to which it belongs.

2. In the June 1955 "Hearings Before the Subcommittees of the Committee on Appropriations, House of Representatives," there were two different sets of figures given regarding cultural expenditures by the Soviets. On page 382 of the Congressional Record the following figures were given: $150 million for cultural propaganda in France alone, with 2,000 artists touring there. During those same hearings, on page 412, Adam Clayton Powell, Jr. told the Committee: "The French Cultural Minister told me in Paris last year that over 1,000 artists from behind the Iron Curtain had come to France in the past two years."

3. The papers of C.D. Jackson are housed at the Eisenhower Library in Abilene, Kansas. The finding aid, *Historical Materials in the Dwight D. Eisenhower Library*, gives Jackson's biography as follows: "Jackson, C.D., Executive, Time Incorporated, 1931–1964; President, Council for Democracy, 1940; Deputy Chief, Psychological Warfare Branch, Allied Forces Headquarters, 1943; Deputy Chief, Psychological Warfare Division, Supreme Headquarters, Allied Expeditionary Force, 1944–1945; President, Free Europe Committee, 1951–1952; Speechwriter for Dwight D. Eisenhower, 1952; Special Assistant to the President for International Affairs, 1952" (p. 22). There is also a discussion of Jackson in Cary Reich's *The Life of Nelson A. Rockefeller* (New York: Doubleday, 1996): "In Eisenhower, Jackson saw a leader 'who grasps the concept of political warfare'; for him it was a way of maintaining power and victory without military fighting. When Rockefeller took Jackson's place as special advisor he took the same position" (p. 553).

4. These comments were made during the "Hearings Before the Committee on Foreign Affairs, House of Representatives, Eighty-Fourth Congress," First Session, 16 Feb. 1955.

5. Martin Walker, *The Cold War, A History* (New York: Holt, 1993), p. 95.

6. *Ibid.*, p. 96.

7. William K. Klingaman, *Encyclopedia of the McCarthy Era* (New York: Facts on File, 1996), pp. 434–435. David Halberstam, in *The Fifties* (New York: Villard Books, 1993), reproduces a slightly different version of McCarthy's speech (p. 50). In Halberstam's version McCarthy talks about a "list of 205 people known to the Secretary of State as being members of the Communist Party." Klingaman notes that "there is still controversy over the precise text of the speech as delivered" (p. 434). He prints the version entered in the *Congressional Record*.

8. Joseph W. Alsop, *"I've Seen the Best of It"* (New York: Norton, 1992), p. 355.

9. Halberstam, *The Fifties*, p. 252.

10. Frank A. Ninkovich, *The Diplomacy of Ideas, U.S. Foreign Policy and Cultural Relations, 1938–1950* (Cambridge: Cambridge University Press, 1981). There is extensive discussion of this issue throughout the book.

11. J. Manuel Espinosa, *Inter-American Beginnings of U.S. Cultural Diplomacy, 1936–1948* (Department of State Publications 8854, International Information and Cultural Series 110, released Dec. 1976), p. 175.

12. Bernard Taper, *Balanchine, A Biography* (New York: Times Books, 1984), pp. 197–198. A revised edition was published in 1996 by the University of California Press.

13. In 1961 a study begun in 1960 was completed regarding the "participation of

American students in the creative and performing arts under the Smith-Mundt and Fulbright programs." The issues in the study had to do with the small numbers involved in arts exchange because of inadequate or inappropriate selection criteria and a lack of information regarding overseas host institutions. The study is dated 1 August 1961 and is at ABECA.

14. The United States established a program of exchange with China that existed from 1942 to 1949. The emphasis was on assisting the Chinese with education, public health, sanitation, agriculture, and engineering. American specialists were sent to China, but there is no record of anyone representing the arts. In 1946–1947 two Chinese artists were invited to the U.S.—the dramatist Chia-Piao Wan and the painter and cartoonist Chien-Yu Yeh.

15. Henry J. Kellerman, *Cultural Relations As An Instrument of U.S. Foreign Policy, The Educational Exchange Program Between the United States and Germany, 1945–54* (Department of State Publication 8931, International Information and Cultural Series 114, released Mar. 1978), p. 3.

16. *Ibid.*, p. 126.

17. ABECA. The reviews are with the material on the Berlin Festivals. They are part of a Foreign Service dispatch to the Department of State dated 15 September 1952 and stamped 25 September 1952. The subject of the dispatch is "Interim Report on Berlin Cultural Festival of 1952."

18. Kellerman, *Cultural Relations,* p. 127.

19. ABECA. This report is with the materials on the Berlin Festivals; it is dated 29 December 1952 and bears the title "Evaluation Report of the Berlin Cultural Festival."

20. Kellerman, *Cultural Relations,* p. 161.

21. Paul Tassovin, "London Notebook," *Dance Observer*, Mar. 1956, p. 40.

22. Joan Lawson, "Moscow State Folk Dancers," *The Dancing Times*, Dec. 1955, p. 142.

Starting Out

1. Alvin Schulman, "The Modern Dance Goes to South America," *Dance Observer* (Mar. 1955), p. 33.

2. ABECA.

3. Hearing before the Subcommittee on Foreign Affairs, House of Representatives, Eighty-Fourth Congress, First Session, 16 Feb. 1955.

4. John Martin, "The Dance: Diplomacy," *The New York Times*, 23 Jan. 1955, sec. 2, p. 11. Actually, Limón was seven years old when he left Mexico.

5. Pauline Koner, *Solitary Song* (Durham, N.C.: Duke University Press, 1989), p. 214.

6. Quaoted in Barbara Pollack and Charles Humphrey Woodford, *Dance is a Moment* (Pennington, N.J.: Princeton Book Company, 1993), p. 36.

7. Koner, *Solitary Song,* pp. 213–214.

8. Hearings before the Subcommittee of the Committee on Appropriations, House of Representatives, Eighty-Fourth Congress, First Session, June 1955. All references to the June 1955 hearings are based on these records, and there will be no further citations in the following section.

9. Rooney was born in Brooklyn in 1903, graduated from Fordham University in 1925, and served as Assistant District Attorney in Brooklyn from 1940 to

1944. He was elected as a Democrat to the 78th Congress to fill the seat opened by the death of Thomas Cullen, and was reelected to the 79th Congress and twelve additional terms. He served from 1944 to 1971.

10. The story was published on 22 December 1954. The excerpts from newspaper articles about *Porgy and Bess* are quoted from the June 1955 Congressional hearings.

11. The story about the La Scala manager and the quotation from Richard Coe are in the June 1955 hearings.

12. *Ibid.*

13. Letter from Robert Schnitzer, General Manager for ANTA of the International Exchange Program, to Nelson Rockefeller, 22 Mar. 1955. This letter contained a summary of reports and excerpts from articles about the *Porgy and Bess* tour.

ANTA, the Dance Panel, and Martha Graham

1. ABECA.

2. ABECA.

3. Breen-ANTA Collection, Special Collections and Archives, Fenwick Library, George Mason University. There is extensive correspondence regarding the frustrations of getting State Department help and the problems faced by Robert Breen and Blevins Davis in this regard. All quotations about the 1950, 1951, and 1953 Ballet Theatre tours are from this collection.

4. The letter to Truman, the State Department telegram, and the Davis-Breen letter are in the Breen-ANTA Collection.

5. ABECA. All letters, reports, documents, and Dance Panel minutes referred to in the remainder of this chapter are housed at the University of Arkansas, unless otherwise noted.

6. "Dance Critic Declines to Serve on Advisory Panel of International Program," *Dance News*, Jan. 1955, p. 1. This article is unsigned.

7. "The President's News Conference of April 7, 1954," *Public Papers of the Presidents, Dwight D. Eisenhower, 1954* (Washington, D.C.: Office of the Federal Register, National Archives Record Service, General Services Administration, 1960), pp. 381–389.

8. *Ibid.*, pp. 382–383.

9. Russell H. Fifield, *Americans in Southeast Asia* (New York: Crowell, 1973), p. 247.

10. *Ibid.*, p. 248.

11. India became independent in 1947, Burma in 1948, Indonesia in 1949.

12. Other works taken on tour were *Dark Meadow* (1946), *Errand into the Maze* (1947), *Canticle for Innocent Comedians* (1952), *Voyage* (1953), and *Ardent Song* (1954).

13. "More News from the Martha Graham 'ANTA' Tour," *Dance Observer*, Mar. 1956, p. 41.

14. Graham's company consisted of sixteen dancers: Helen McGehee, Ethel Winter, Linda Hodes, Matt Turney, Ellen Van Der Hoeven, Esta McKayle, Christine Lawson, Marian Sarach, Robert Cohan, Stuart Hodes, Bertram Ross, David Wood, Donald McKayle, Donya Feuer, Ellen Siegel, and Paul Taylor. Pianist Cameron McCosh also traveled with the company. Three of the dancers— Turney, Lawson, and McKayle—were African-Americans.

15. "News Items from Martha Graham's 'ANTA' Tour," *Dance Observer*, Feb. 1956, pp. 24–25; "More News from the Martha Graham 'ANTA' Tour," *Dance Observer*, Mar. 1956, p. 41.
16. Quoted in Don McDonagh, *Martha Graham, A Biography* (New York: Praeger, 1973), pp. 244–245.

The Avant-Garde Conundrum

1. ABECA. All minutes of Dance Panel meetings are in this collection.
2. In 1947, under the auspices of Ballet Society, Kirstein presented Merce Cunningham's first ballet, *The Seasons*. The work had music by John Cage and sets by Isamu Noguchi. See David Vaughan, "Merce Cunningham's *The Seasons*," *Dance Chronicle*, 18, no. 2 (1995), pp. 311–318.
3. Harry Partch (1901–1976) was known as an experimental composer. He rejected Western scales and techiques, and invented his own instruments.
4. Merce Cunningham, "Two Questions and Five Dances," *Dance Perspectives*, no. 34 (Summer 1968), p. 49.
5. *Ibid.*, p. 51.
6. Quoted in "Nik, A Documentary," ed. Marcia Siegel, *Dance Perspectives*, no. 48 (Winter 1971), p. 9.
7. *Ibid.*, pp. 9–10.
8. *Ibid.*, p. 11.
9. Agnes de Mille, *Dance to the Piper* (Boston: Little, Brown, 1952), pp. 261–262.
10. Erick Hawkins, *The Body is a Clear Place and Other Statements on Dance* (Pennington, N.J.: Princeton Book Company, 1992), p. 54. This particular essay by Hawkins is dated 4 January 1962.
11. Edwin Denby, *Dance Writings* (New York: Knopf, 1986), p. 287.
12. Walter Terry, *I Was There* (New York: Marcel Dekker, 1978), p. 232.
13. Denby, *Dance Writings*, pp. 405–406.
14. Her name is now "Anna" Halprin. In *Moving Toward Life* (Hanover, N.H.: Wesleyan University Press/University Press of New England, 1995), she writes: "After my operation for cancer, I had an occasion to look at my birth certificate and noticed, to my surprise, that my name was Hannah Deborah, after my mother's mother. I was working with a multiracial company at the same time, and reclaiming our heritage was a big part of our philosophy. Many people in the group were changing their names, and it was an important time for me to change mine. I changed my name from the Anglo-Saxon 'Ann' to the much more Jewish 'Anna.' I was Ann Halprin until 1972" (p. 75).
15. *Ibid.*, pp. 84–85.

Ballet and the Soviet-American Exchange

1. Extensive information on the *Porgy and Bess* tour is available in the Breen-ANTA Collection, Special Collections and Archives, Fenwick Library, George Mason University.
2. Boston Symphony Orchestra Archives, Symphony Hall, Boston. In 1952 the Boston Symphony was funded by the Congress for Cultural Freedom, which in its turn was funded by the Central Intelligence Agency (CIA), to participate in a massive propaganda effort held in Paris, the Festival of the Twenti-

eth-Century Arts. Other participants in the Festival were the Vienna State Opera, New York City Ballet, the chorus and orchestra of the Academy of St. Cecilia in Rome, and France's Conservatory Orchestra. Explained *The New York Herald Tribune* on 20 January 1952: "One of the principal motives of the Congress in sponsoring the spring festival, it was said, is to combat the current Communist party line in Europe which has been insulting Western art and culture as 'decadent.'" The article noted that the cost for the 104-member orchestra was "estimated from $150,000 to $175,000." For further information about the Congress for Cultural Freedom, see Peter Coleman, *The Liberal Conspiracy, The Congress for Cultural Freedom and the Struggle for the Mind of Postwar Europe* (London: Macmillan, 1989). The information on this particular Festival is on pp. 55–56. After the Paris Festival, the orchestra performed in Holland, Belgium, Germany, England, and some other cities in France.

3. Harlow Robinson, *The Last Impresario* (New York: Viking, 1994). This biography of Hurok contains information on the Gilels and Oistrakh tours (pp. 344–345), the Stern and Peerce tours (pp. 350–351), and the Rostropovich tour (p. 343).

4. B.J. Cutler, "Russians Won't Submit to U.S. Fingerprinting," *The New York Herald Tribune*, 1 June 1956.

5. In *The Last Impresario*, Robinson discusses Hurok's efforts at length (pp. 347–357); there is also considerable information on the Moiseyev's 1958 tour (pp. 358–367).

6. The unsigned article, dated 2 May 1958, went on to comment: "The 'cold war' notwithstanding, the Russians have the hottest show in town. For the most bitter competition here in recent days has been for tickets to the Moiseyev Dance Company."

7. Lydia Joel, "The Moiseyev Dance Company," *Dance Magazine*, June 1958, pp. 30–33, 57.

8. The Moiseyev clipping file at the Dance Collection, New York Public Library for the Performing Arts, has hundreds of articles about the 1958 tour.

9. Albert Goldberg, "Sensational Moiseyev Dancers Will Open to Shrine Sellout Saturday," *The Los Angeles Times*, 18 May 1958. The article begins by saying: "The biggest terpsichorean sensation to hit this country since the Diaghilev ballet in 1915 [sic], the Moiseyev Dance Company is due to arrive in Shrine Auditorium Saturday night."

10. Max de Schauensee, "Moiseyev Dancers Win Ovation Here," *Philadelphia Bulletin*, 13 June 1958.

11. Gloria Emerson, "Soviet Dancers' Shopping Leads to Beauty Salon," *The New York Times*, 23 Apr. 1958.

12. Lawrence Fellows, "U.S. Dancers Teach Russians Ins and Outs of Virginia Reel," *The New York Times*, 28 Apr. 1958.

13. Jack Gould, "TV: Moiseyev Dancers," *The New York Times*, 30 June 1958.

14. Jack Gould, "TV Notebook," *The New York Times*, 6 July 1958.

15. Program for 11 and 12 June 1958, Moiseyev Dance Company, City of Philadelphia, Moiseyev Clipping File, Dance Collection.

16. *Bluebeard*, choreographed by Michel Fokine in 1941, "was the first ballet created especially for Ballet Theatre that proved to be a critical and popular success. It was still in the repertory when the company visited the Soviet Union in 1960, where it was seen by Premier Nikita S. Khrushchev, who declared it

to be his favorite of the evening's programs" (Charles Payne, *American Ballet Theatre* [New York: Knopf, 1978], p. 69).

17. Maria Tallchief, with Larry Kaplan, *Maria Tallchief* (New York: Henry Holt, 1997), pp. 261–262.
18. *Ibid.*, p. 262.
19. *Ibid.*, p. 260. For the Nureyev incident, see John Gruen, *Erik Bruhn, Danseur Noble* (New York: Viking, 1979), p. 100.
20. Lincoln Kirstein, *Thirty Years, The New York City Ballet* (New York: Knopf, 1978), p. 175.
21. Allegra Kent, *Once a Dancer* (New York: St. Martin's Press, 1997), p. 157.
22. Kirstein, *Thirty Years,* p. 171.
23. *Ibid.*
24. Kent, *Once a Dancer*, pp. 156–157.
25. Kirstein calls this theater the Palace of the Soviets; Kent the Palace of the Congresses. In the Dance Panel minutes of 20 December 1962 it is referred to as the Hall of Congress.
26. Kirstein, *Thirty Years*, p. 175.
27. Kent, *Once a Dancer*, p. 160.
28. *Ibid.*, p. 164.
29. This report is part of the New York City Ballet file, Special Collections, University of Arkansas.
30. *Ibid.*
31. Sasha Anawalt, *The Joffrey Ballet: Robert Joffrey and the Making of an American Dance Company* (New York: Scribner, 1996), p. 179.

African-American Artists

1. ABECA.
2. Quoted in Arthur Todd, "Two Way Passage for Dance," *Dance Magazine*, July 1962, p. 40.
3. Alvin Ailey, with A. Peter Bailey, *Revelations: The Autobiography of Alvin Ailey* (New York: Carol Publishing Group, 1995), p. 51.
4. Jennifer Dunning, *Alvin Ailey: A Life in Dance* (New York: Addison-Wesley, 1996), p. 89.
5. Doris Hering, "Alvin Ailey and Company, Ernest Parham and Company," *Dance Magazine*, May 1958, p. 65.
6. H[arry] B[ernstein], "Alvin Ailey and Company," *Dance Observer*, Feb. 1959, p. 25. This is a review of the performance at the Ninety-Second Street Y on 21 December 1958.
7. Hering, p. 65.
8. Bernstein, pp. 24–25.
9. *Ibid.*, p. 24.
10. Unless otherwise noted, all comments referring to Dance Panel meetings are from the minutes.
11. I am grateful to Don Martin, one of the dancers, for allowing me to consult his collection of programs, menus, airline tickets, and other materials from the tour.
12. Arthur Todd, "Two Way Passage for Dance," *Dance Magazine*, July 1962, p. 40. Jennifer Dunning, in *Alvin Ailey* (p. 145), calls the Tetley dance *Mountainway Chant.*

13. ABECA.
14. ABECA. The report was a foreign service dispatch from the American Embassy in Saigon and dated 21 May 1962. All quotations are from this same report.
15. Ailey, *Revelations*, p. 51.
16. Joyce Aschenbrenner, *Katherine Dunham: Reflections on the Social and Political Contexts of Afro-American Dance*, Dance Research Annual, no. 12 (New York: Congress on Research in Dance, 1981), p. 12. Constance Valis Hill gives 1944 for the founding of Dunham's school ("Katherine Dunham's *Southland*: Protest in the Face of Repression," *Dance Research Journal*, 26, no. 2 [Fall 1994], p. 1).
17. Katherine Dunham, *Journey to Accompong* (New York: Henry Holt, 1946). Her articles published in the 1940s included "The Negro Dance," in *The Negro Caravan*, ed. Sterling Brown, Arthur P. Davis, and Ulysses Lee (New York: Dryden Press, 1941), and "Las Danzas de Haití," *Actua Anthropologica*, Nov. 1947.
18. Katherine Dunham, "Program: *Southland* in Santiago de Chile, World Premiere, January 1951," in *Kaiso! Katherine Dunham: An Anthology of Writings*, ed. VèVè A. Clark and Margaret B. Wilkerson (Berkeley: Institute for the Study of Social Change, CCEW Women's Center, University of California-Berkeley, 1978), p. 118.
19. Valis Hill, p. 5.
20. *Ibid*. Valis Hill discusses at length Dunham's reluctance to keep this work in repertory, not only because of negative reviews from critics, but also because her own dancers were reluctant to perform such an angry piece. They felt that with its extensive touring schedule, the company allowed them to avoid racial issues, and they were not eager to put themselves in a difficult position.
21. Terry Harnan, *African Rhythm, American Dance* (New York: Knopf, 1974). Chapters 12 and 13 (pp. 155–184) contain a lengthy discussion of Dunham's activities and problems in the late 1950s.
22. Dave Jampel, "Left to Her Own Resources In Global Touring, Katherine Dunham Gibes at Robert Schnitzer of ANTA," *International Variety*, 7 May 1958. This was part of an article datelined April 29 and written from Tokyo.
23. *Ibid*.
24. For a summary of critical opinion of Dunham and her work, see Valis Hill, p. 1.
25. ABECA. This airgram, dated 24 October 1962, was written by J. Carson, a chargé d'affaires at the American Embassy in Cotonou, to the Department of State.
26. ABECA. This airgram, dated 17 January 1963, was sent to the Department of State by Joseph N. Greene, Jr., a Counselor at the U.S. Embassy in Lagos. Some performers were received positively by him, including the folk singer Odetta, jazz dancers Al Minns and Leon James, and folk singer Brock Peters.
27. Margaret Lloyd, *The Borzoi Book of Modern Dance* (1949; rpt. New York: Dance Horizons, [1969?]), p. 245.
28. Barbara Stratyner, *Ned Wayburn and the Dance Routine*, Studies in Dance History, no. 13 (1996).
29. Josephine Rudnick, "George Tapps in Africa," *Dance Magazine*, Oct. 1962, pp. 19–21. The dancers who toured with Tapps were Vivian Burns, Marlene DiNapoli, Hu Pope, and Joseph Ward Russell; the musicans were Patricia Melville and Wynn Bass, and the stage manager was William Walters.

30. ABECA. A foreign service dispatch, dated 26 March 1962, from the American Embassy in Accra to the Department of State, gives information on Tapps's teaching activities.

How Broad a Spectrum?

1. Only two groups were finally considered—one from Bennington College and the Juilliard Dance Theatre. All the other college groups were rejected. Martha Hill actively pressed for the Juilliard Dance Theatre to be supported by the program; it was given first priority as a professional student group, and Bennington was considered a close second. Neither group was sent abroad.
2. Sophie Maslow, a member of the Martha Graham company in the late 1930s and early 1940s, helped found the Dudley-Maslow-Bales Dance Trio in 1942. In March 1942 she created *Folksay*, a piece that incorporated folk songs such as "On Top of Old Smokey" and "Sweet Betsy From Pike," with narration taken from Carl Sandburg's *The People, Yes*. Doris Humphrey's *Shakers*, first performed in 1931, was based on the religious dances of the Shakers. *Games*, created by Donald McKayle in 1951, was based on street games he remembered growing up as an African-American child in New York City.
3. Paul Rawlings, "Close-up of Bambi Linn and Rod Alexander," *Dance Magazine*, June 1958, pp. 27–29, 54. The Dance Collection has an extensive clipping file on Rod Alexander.
4. The Rod Alexander clipping file at the Dance Collection has *Dance Jubilee* programs from Burma, India, Iran, Lebanon, and Thailand. In Bambi Linn's clipping file there is a program for a performance in Larchmont, New York, sponsored by the Community Concert Association. At the bottom of the program, there is a note indicating that the group was managed by Columbia Artists. There is no specific date on the program, but a handwritten note indicates that it was during the 1958–1959 season. At this point, obviously, the couple was still working together. Wakefield Poole, a dancer on the tour, wrote a series of letters from different cities published in *Dance Magazine* under the title "Wonderful Release from Earnestness" (May 1960, pp. 34–38, 64–68).
5. It is not clear why the program note was so specific about the year, rather than linking swing to the 1930s in general.
6. The publication in the late 1960s of *Jazz Dance: The Story of American Vernacular Dance* by Marshall and Jean Stearns (New York: Macmillan, 1968) was instrumental in demonstrating to a broad public the African-American influences on popular dance forms.

On the Home Front

1. Hearings, Committee on Public Works and Subcommittee on Public Buildings and Grounds, 22 Apr. l958.
2. *Ibid.*
3. According to the biographical information presented at the hearing, Dowling had business interests in both New York and Washington. He was the president and director of the City Investing Company and a director of Starrett Brothers and Eken. His business firms had interests in Washington's National and Dupont Theatres. Dowling was considered an excellent fundraiser. In his work with ANTA and the international exchange program, he had raised

$400,000 for the "Salute to France" in May and June 1955, when the Philadelphia Orchestra, the New York City Ballet, and productions of *Medea* and *Oklahoma!* were sent to Paris. This was a private-public venture: the government gave $100,000, and Dowling raised another $300,000.

4. Gary O. Larson, *The Reluctant Patron: The United States Government and the Arts, 1943–1965* (Philadelphia: University of Pennsylvania Press, 1983), p. 136.

5. Stevens was a very successful and wealthy real estate developer and Broadway producer. He was well-connected and an experienced fundraiser for cultural events and for the Democratic Party.

6. Heckscher was a former editorial writer for *The New York Herald Tribune*. During the 1950s he served on the Museum of Modern Art's International Council and on the New York City Art Commission.

7. The members of the first National Council on the Arts were the actress Elizabeth Ashley, the writer Ralph Ellison, Father Gilbert Hartke, the head of the Speech and Drama Department at Catholic University, the fashion designer Eleanor Lambert, the actor Gregory Peck, Otto Wittmann, the director of the Toledo Museum of Art, and the author and publisher Stanley Young.

8. For a history of the struggle by Congressional advocates to secure domestic support for the arts from the 1940s to the early 1960s, see Livingston Biddle, *Our Government and the Arts* (New York: American Council for the Arts, 1988); Stephen Benedict, ed., *Public Money and the Muse* (New York: Norton, 1991); and Larson, *The Reluctant Patron*, cited above.

9. ABECA.

10. ABECA.

1955 Lucia Chase, director, Ballet Theatre Foundation
Emily Coleman, music and dance editor, *Newsweek*
Agnes de Mille, choreographer, New York (joined October 1955)
Hyman Faine, executive secretary, American Guild of Musical Artists
Martha Hill, director, Dance Department, Juilliard School of Music
Doris Humphrey, teacher and choreographer, New York
Lincoln Kirstein, general director, New York City Ballet
Walter Terry, dance critic, *The New York Herald Tribune*
Bethsabée de Rothschild, director, Rothschild Foundation

1956 George Beiswanger, teacher and dance writer, Atlanta
Lucia Chase, director, Ballet Theatre Foundation
Emily Coleman, music and dance editor, *Newsweek*
Agnes de Mille, choreographer, New York
Hyman Faine, executive secretary, American Guild of Musical Artists
Alfred Frankenstein, music and art editor, *The San Francisco Chronicle*
Martha Hill, director, Dance Department, Juilliard School of Music
Doris Humphrey, teacher and choreographer, New York
Lincoln Kirstein, general director, New York City Ballet
Margaret Lloyd, dance critic, *The Christian Science Monitor*
John Rosenfield, theater editor and music critic, *The Dallas Morning News*
Bethsabée de Rothschild, director, Rothschild Foundation
  (resigned December 1956)
Walter Terry, dance critic, *The New York Herald Tribune*

1957 Ann Barzel, dance critic, *Chicago American*
George Beiswanger, teacher and dance writer, Atlanta
Lucia Chase, director, Ballet Theatre Foundation
Emily Coleman, music and dance editor, *Newsweek*
Agnes de Mille, choreographer, New York
Hyman Faine, executive secretary, American Guild of Musical Artists
Alfred Frankenstein, music and art editor, *The San Francisco Chronicle*

Martha Hill, director, Dance Department, Juilliard School of Music

Doris Humphrey, teacher and choreographer, New York

Lincoln Kirstein, general director, New York City Ballet

Margaret Lloyd, dance critic, *The Christian Science Monitor*

John Rosenfield, theater editor and music critic, *The Dallas Morning News*

Walter Terry, dance critic, *The New York Herald Tribune*

1958 Ann Barzel, dance critic, *Chicago American*

George Beiswanger, teacher and dance writer, Atlanta

Lucia Chase, director, Ballet Theatre Foundation

Emily Coleman, music and dance editor, *Newsweek*

Agnes de Mille, choreographer, New York

Hyman Faine, executive secretary, American Guild of Musical Artists

Alfred Frankenstein, music and art editor, *The San Francisco Chronicle*

Martha Hill, director, Dance Department, Juilliard School of Music

Doris Humphrey, teacher and choreographer, New York
  (died December 1958)

Lincoln Kirstein, general director, New York City Ballet

Margaret Lloyd, dance critic, *The Christian Science Monitor*

John Rosenfield, theater editor and music critic, *The Dallas Morning News*

Walter Terry, dance critic, *The New York Herald Tribune*

1959 Ann Barzel, dance critic, *Chicago American*

George Beiswanger, teacher and dance writer, Atlanta

Lucia Chase, director, Ballet Theatre Foundation

Emily Coleman, music and dance editor, *Newsweek*

Agnes de Mille, choreographer, New York

Hyman Faine, executive secretary, American Guild of Musical Artists

Alfred Frankenstein, music and art editor, *The San Francisco Chronicle*

Martha Hill, director, Dance Department, Juilliard School of Music

Lincoln Kirstein, general director, New York City Ballet

Margaret Lloyd, dance critic, *The Christian Science Monitor*

John Rosenfield, theater editor and music critic, *The Dallas Morning News*

Walter Terry, dance critic, *The New York Herald Tribune*

1960 William Bales, choreographer and teacher, New York
  (joined November 1960)

Ann Barzel, dance critic, *Chicago American*

George Beiswanger, teacher and dance writer, Atlanta

Lucia Chase, director, Ballet Theatre Foundation (resigned summer 1960)

Emile Coleman, music and dance editor, *Newsweek*

Agnes de Mille, choreographer, New York

Hyman Faine, executive secretary, American Guild of Musical Artists

Alfred Frankenstein, music and art editor, *The San Francisco Chronicle*

Martha Hill, director, Dance Department, Juilliard School of Music

Lincoln Kirstein, general director, New York City Ballet
  (resigned January 1960)

William Kolodney, educational director, Ninety-Second Street Y

Margaret Lloyd, dance critic, *The Christian Science Monitor*
  (died February 1960)

John Rosenfield, theater editor and music critic, *The Dallas Morning News*

Walter Terry, dance critic, *The New York Herald Tribune*

1961 William Bales, choreographer and teacher, New York

Ann Barzel, dance critic, *Chicago American*

George Beiswanger, teacher and dance writer, Atlanta

Emily Coleman, music and dance editor, *Newsweek*

Agnes de Mille, choreographer, New York

Hyman Faine, executive secretary, American Guild of Musical Artists

Alfred Frankenstein, music and art editor, *The San Francisco Chronicle*

Martha Hill, director, Dance Department, Juilliard School of Music

William Kolodney, educational director, Ninety-Second Street Y

John Rosenfield, theater editor and music critic, *The Dallas Morning News*

Walter Terry, dance critic, *The New York Herald Tribune*

1962 William Bales, choreographer and teacher, New York

Ann Barzel, dance critic, *Chicago American*

George Beiswanger, teacher and dance writer, Atlanta

Isadora Bennett, dance publicist, New York

Emily Coleman, music and dance editor, *Newsweek*

Agnes de Mille, choreographer, New York

Hyman Faine, executive secretary, American Guild of Musical Artists

Alfred Frankenstein, music and art editor, *The San Francisco Chronicle*

Martha Hill, director, Dance Department, Juilliard School of Music

Hanya Holm, choreographer, New York

William Kolodney, educational director, Ninety-Second Street Y

Lillian Moore, teacher, historian, and dance writer, New York

John Rosenfield, theater editor and music critic, *The Dallas Morning News*

Walter Terry, dance critic, *The New York Herald Tribune*

Special Collections

American National Theatre and Academy Archives, George Mason University Libraries, Fairfax, Virginia.
Boston Symphony Orchestra Archives, Symphony Hall, Boston.
Bureau of Educational and Historical and Cultural Affairs Historical Collection, Special Collections Division, University of Arkansas Libraries, Fayetteville, Arkansas.
Eisenhower Library, Abilene, Kansas.
The New York Public Library for the Performing Arts, Dance Collection.
United States Information Agency Historical Collection.

Congressional Hearings

U.S. Congress, House. Committee on Foreign Affairs. *United States Information Agency*. Hearings 16 Feb. 1955, 84 Cong. 1 Sess. Washington, D.C.: Government Printing Office, 1955.
U.S. Congress, House. Subcommittees of the Committee on Appropriations. (*Emergency Fund for International Affairs, Executive*, pp. 272-408.) *The Supplemental Appropriations Bill, 1956*. Hearings 13, 14, and 20 June 1955, 84 Cong. 1 Sess. Washington, D.C.: Government Printing Office, 1955.
U.S. Congress, Senate. Committee on Foreign Relations. *International Cultural Exchange and Trade Fair Participation Act of 1956*, S. 3116 and S. 3172. Hearings 21 Feb. 1956, 84 Cong. 2 Sess. Washington, D.C.: Government Printing Office, 1956.
U.S. Congress, House. Subcommittee of the Committee on Appropriations; Subcommittee on Departments of State and Justice and the Judiciary and Related Agencies Appropriations. *Departments of State and Justice, The Judiciary, and Related Agencies Appropriations for 1957*. Hearings 14 Mar. 1956, 84 Cong. 2 Sess. Washington, D.C.: Government Printing Office, 1956.
U.S. Congress, Senate. Subcommittee on Public Works. *Public Buildings*, S. 1985, S. 3335, S. 3560. Hearings 22 and 23 April 1958, 85 Cong. 2 Sess. (S. 3335 was the bill to create a National Center for the Performing Arts.) Washington, D.C.: Government Printing Office, 1958.
U.S. Congress, House. Subcommittee on Buildings and Grounds of the Committee on Public Works. *Public Buildings*. Hearings 5 Aug. 1958, 85 Cong. 2 Sess. Washington, D.C.: Government Printing Office, 1958.

Books and Articles

Ailey, Alvin, with A. Peter Bailey. *Revelations: The Autobiography of Alvin Ailey*. New York: Carol Publishing Group, 1995.

Alsop, Joseph W., with Adam Platt. *"I've Seen the Best of It."* New York: Norton, 1992.

Ambrose, Stephen E. *Eisenhower, Soldier and President*. New York: Touchstone, 1990.

———. *Rise to Globalism: American Foreign Policy, 1938–1980*. New York: Penguin, 1980.

Anawalt, Sasha. *The Joffrey Ballet: Robert Joffrey and the Making of an American Dance Company*. New York: Scribner, 1996.

Anderson, Jack. *The One and Only: The Ballet Russe de Monte Carlo*. New York: Dance Horizons, 1981.

Arndt, Richard T., and David Lee Rubin. *The Fulbright Difference, 1948-1992*. New Brunswick: Transaction Publishers, 1993.

Aschenbrenner, Joyce. *Katherine Dunham: Reflections on the Social and Political Contexts of Afro-American Dance*. Dance Research Annual, no. 12. New York: Congress on Research in Dance, 1981.

Balfe, Judith H., and Margaret Jane Wyszomirski. *Art, Ideology and Politics*. New York: Praeger, 1985.

Banes, Sally. *Greenwich Village 1963: Avant-Garde Performance and the Effervescent Body*. Durham: Duke University Press, 1993.

———. *Terpsichore in Sneakers, Post-Modern Dance*. Boston: Houghton Mifflin, 1980.

Beckford, Ruth. *Katherine Dunham, A Biography*. New York: Dekker, 1979.

Benedict, Stephen, ed. *Public Money and the Muse: Essays on Government Funding for the Arts*. New York: Norton, 1991.

Biddle, Livingston. *Our Government and the Arts: A Perspective from the Inside*. New York: American Council for the Arts, 1988.

Biskind, Peter. *Seeing is Believing: How Hollywood Taught Us to Stop Worrying and Love the Fifties*. New York: Pantheon Books, 1983.

Bissell, Robyn. "Daniel Nagrin's Path Abroad, 1967." *Proceedings of the Society of Dance History Scholars*, 1992, pp. 11-20.

Blum, Robert, ed. *Cultural Affairs and Foreign Relations*. Englewood Cliffs, N.J.: Prentice-Hall, [1963].

Boardman, Gerald. *American Musical Theatre*. New York: Oxford University Press, 1978.

Braden, Thomas W. "I'm Glad the CIA is 'Immoral.'" *The Saturday Evening Post*, 20 May 1967, p. 10.

Braisted, Paul S., ed. *Cultural Affairs and Foreign Relations*. Washington, D.C.: Columbia Books for the American Assembly, 1968.

Branch, Taylor. *Parting the Waters: America in the King Years, 1954-1963*. New York: Simon and Schuster, 1988.

Brown, Sterling, Arthur P. Davis, and Ulysses Lee, eds. *The Negro Caravan*. New York: Dryden Press, 1941.

Buchwalter, Andrew, ed. *Cultural Democracy: Social and Ethical Issues in Public Support for the Arts and Humanities*. Boulder: Westview Press, 1992.

Burgering, Jacques J. "Lucas Hoving: The Circle That Goes Around." M.A. Thesis, American University, 1995.

Cage, John. *Silence*. Middletown, Conn.: Wesleyan University Press, 1973.

Carbaugh, Donal, ed. *Cultural Communication and Intercultural Contact*. London: Lawrence Erlbaum Associates, 1990.

Cavaliero, R. and E. "Cultural Diplomacy: The Diplomacy of Influence." *The Round Table*, no. 298 (Apr. 1986), pp. 139-144.

Chun, Myung Hye. "The United States Government's Cultural Presentation Program in Korea." M.A. Thesis, American University, 1993.

Clark, VèVè A., and Margaret B. Wilkerson, eds. *Kaiso! Katherine Dunham: An Anthology of Writings*. Berkeley: Institute for the Study of Social Change, CCEW Women's Center, University of California-Berkeley, 1978.

Cockcroft, Eva. "Abstract Expressionism: Weapon of the Cold War," *Artforum*, 12 (June 1974), pp. 39-41.

Cohen, Selma Jeanne, ed. *Doris Humphrey, An Artist First*. Middletown, Conn.: Wesleyan University Press, 1972.

Coleman, Peter. *The Liberal Conspiracy: The Congress for Cultural Freedom and the Struggle for the Mind of Postwar Europe*. London: Macmillan, 1989.

Coombs, Philip. *The Fourth Dimension of Foreign Policy: Educational and Cultural Affairs*. New York: Harper and Row, 1964.

Cummings, Milton C., Jr., and Richard S. Katz, eds. *The Patron State: Government and the Arts in Europe, North American and Japan*. New York: Oxford University Press, 1987.

Cunningham, Merce. *Changes: Notes on Choreography*. New York: Something Else Press, 1968.

———. "Two Questions and Five Dances." *Dance Perspectives*, no. 34 (Summer 1968).

Dances on a Plane: Cage, Cunningham, Johns. New York: Knopf, 1990. This was published in association with the Anthony d'Offay Gallery.

Davison, W. Phillips. *International Political Communication*. New York: Praeger, 1965.

De Mille, Agnes. *Dance to the Piper*. Boston: Little, Brown, 1952.

———. *Martha: The Life and Work of Martha Graham*. New York: Random House, 1991.

———. *Portrait Gallery*. Boston: Houghton Mifflin, 1990.

Denby, Edwin. *Dance Writings*. Ed. Robert Cornfield and William Mackay. New York: Knopf, 1986.

Diggins, John Patrick. *The Proud Decades: America in War and Peace, 1941-1960*. New York: Norton, 1988.

Doss, Erika. *Benton, Pollock, and the Politics of Modernism From Regionalism to Abstract Expressionism*. Chicago: University of Chicago Press, 1991.

Dudden, Arthur Power, and Russell Dynes, eds. *The Fulbright Experience 1946-1986*. New Brunswick, N.J.: Transaction Books, 1987.

Dunham, Katherine. *A Touch of Innocence: Memoirs of Childhood*. Chicago: University of Chicago Press, 1994.

———. *Island Possessed*. Chicago: University of Chicago Press, 1994.

———. *Journey to Accompong*. New York: Holt, 1946.

Dunning, Jennifer. *Alvin Ailey, A Life in Dance*. New York: Addison-Wesley, 1996.

Elder, Robert E. *The Information Machine: The United States Information Agency and American Foreign Policy*. Syracuse: Syracuse University Press, 1968.

Emery, Lynne Fauley. *Black Dance in the United States From 1619 to 1970*. 2nd rev. ed. Princeton: Princeton Book Company, 1988.

Espinosa, J. Manuel. *Inter-American Beginnings of U.S. Cultural Diplomacy 1936-1948*. Department of State Publication 8854. International Information and Cultural Series 110. Released Dec. 1976.

Fairbank, Wilma. *America's Cultural Experiment in China 1942–1949*. Department of State Publication 8839. International Information and Cultural Series 108. Released June 1976.

Fifield, Russell H. *Americans in Southeast Asia*. New York: Crowell, 1973.

Frank, Rusty E. *Tap! The Greatest Tap Dance Stars and Their Stories 1900-1955*. New York: Morrow, 1990.

Frankel, Charles. *High on Foggy Bottom: An Outsider's Inside View of the Government*. New York: Harper and Row, 1968.

———. *The Neglected Aspect of Foreign Affairs: American Educational and Cultural Policy Abroad*. Washington, D.C.: Brookings Institute, 1965.

Fried, Richard M. *Men Against McCarthy*. New York: Columbia University Press, 1976.

Fulbright, J. William. *The Crippled Giant: American Foreign Policy and Its Domestic Consequences*. New York: Random House, 1972.

———, with Seth P. Tillman. *The Price of Empire*. New York: Pantheon, 1989.

Glover, Jean Ruth. "Pearl Primus: Cross-Cultural Pioneer of American Dance." M.A. Thesis, American University, 1989.

Goldman, Erick F. *The Crucial Decade—And After: America, 1945–1960*. New York: Vintage Books, 1960.

Goodman, Walter. *The Committee: The Extraordinary Career of the House Committee on Un-American Activities*. Foreword by Richard H. Rover. New York: Farrar, Straus, and Giroux, 1968.

Graham, Martha. *Blood Memory, An Autobiography*. New York: Doubleday, 1991.

Green, Stanley. *The World of Musical Comedy*. New York: A.S. Barnes, 1980.

Gruen, John. *Erik Bruhn, Danseur Noble*. New York: Viking Press, 1979.

Guilbaut, Serge. *How New York Stole the Idea of Modern Art: Abstract Expressionism, Freedom, and the Cold War*. Trans. Arthur Goldhammer. Chicago: University of Chicago Press, 1983.

Haddow, Robert. *Pavillions of Plenty: Establishing American Culture Abroad in the 1950s*. Washington, D.C.: Smithsonian Institution Press, 1997.

Halberstam, David. *The Fifties*. New York: Villard Books, 1993.

Hanzal, Carla M. "The Fusion of Art and Politics: Events Shaping the Public-Private Venture to Take American Art Abroad." M.A. Thesis, American University, 1990.

Harman, Terry. *African Rhythm, American Dance: A Biography of Katherine Dunham*. New York: Knopf, 1974.

Hawkins, Erick. *The Body is a Clear Place and Other Statements on Dance*. Princeton: Princeton Book Company, 1992.

Henderson, John. *The United States Information Agency*. New York: Praeger, 1969.

Hofstadter, Richard. *Anti-Intellectualism in American Life*. New York: Knopf, 1970.

Howe, Irving. *Steady Work: Essays in the Politics of Democratic Radicalism, 1953-1966*. New York: Harcourt, Brace and World, 1966.

Javits, Senator Jacob K., and Rafael Steinberg. *Javits: The Autobiography of a Public Man*. Boston: Houghton Mifflin, 1981.

John, Mary Widrig. "ANTA: The American National Theatre and Academy, Its First Quarter Century 1935-1960." Diss., New York University, 1965.

Johnson, Haynes, and Bernard M. Gwertzman. *Fulbright, the Dissenter*. New York: Modern Library Editions, 1968.

Kammen, Michael. "Culture and the State in America." *Journal of American History*, 83, no. 3 (Dec. 1996), pp. 791-814.

Kaplan, Rachel, ed. *Anna Halprin, Moving Toward Life: Five Decades of Transformational Dance*. Hanover, N.H.: Wesleyan University Press/University Press of New England, 1995.

Kazan, Elia. *A Life*. New York: Knopf, 1988.

Kellerman, Henry J. *Cultural Relations as an Instrument of U.S. Foreign Policy: The Educational Exchange Program Between the United States and Germany 1945-1954*. Department of State Publication 8931. International Information and Cultural Series 114. Released March 1978.

Kent, Allegra. *Once A Dancer, An Autobiography*. New York: St. Martin's Press, 1997.

Kirstein, Lincoln. *The New York City Ballet*. New York: Knopf, 1973.

———. *Thirty Years: The New York City Ballet*. New York: Knopf, 1978.

Klingaman, William K. *Encyclopedia of the McCarthy Era*. New York: Facts on File, 1996.

Klosty, James, ed. *Merce Cunningham*. New York: Dutton, 1975.

Koner, Pauline. *Solitary Song*. Durham, N.C.: Duke University Press, 1989.

Kostelanetz, Richard. *Merce Cunningham: Dancing in Space and Time*. Pennington, N.J.: A Cappella Books, 1992.

Kraske, Gary E. *Missionaries of the Book: The American Library Association and the Origins of United States Cultural Diplomacy*. Westport, Conn.: Greenwood Press, 1985.

Kreemer, Connie. "What is American Dance?" *Proceedings of the Society of Dance History Scholars*, 1992, pp. 59-68.

Laqueur, Walter. "Save Public Diplomacy." *Foreign Affairs*, 73, no. 5 (Sept. 1994), pp. 19-24.

Larson, Gary O. *The Reluctant Patron: The United States Government and the Arts 1943-1965*. Philadelphia: University of Pennsylvania Press, 1983.

Leatherman, Leroy. *Martha Graham, Portrait of the Lady as an Artist*. New York: Knopf, 1966.

Lederer, William J., and Eugene Burdick. *The Ugly American*. New York: Norton, 1958.

Leuchtenburg, William E. *A Troubled Feast: American Society Since 1945*. Boston: Little, Brown, 1973.

Lloyd, Margaret. *The Borzoi Book of Modern Dance*. New York: Knopf, 1949; rpt. New York: Dance Horizons, [1969?].

Martin, John. *Ruth Page: An Intimate Biography*. New York: Marcel Dekker, 1977.

May, Larry, ed. *Recasting America: Culture and Politics in the Age of Cold War*. Chicago: University of Chicago Press, 1989.

Maguet, Kathryn. "Toward a National Theatre." M.A. Thesis, American University, 1989.

Mathews, Jane DeHart. "Art and Politics in Cold War America." *American Historical Review*, 81, no. 4 (Oct. 1976), pp. 762-787.

Mazo, Joseph H. *The Alvin Ailey Dance Theater*. New York: Morrow, 1978.

McDonagh, Don. *Martha Graham, A Biography*. New York: Praeger, 1973.

Montano, Severino. "The Administrative History of the American National Theatre and Academy." Diss., American University, 1949.

Morizet, Imogen. "The Role of the Arts in International Cultural Exchange from the Perspective of the Japan-United States Friendship Commission." M.A. Thesis, American University, 1994.

Mulcahy, Kevin V., and C. Richard Swaim. *Public Policy and the Arts*. Boulder: Westview Press, 1982.

Mulcahy, Kevin V., and Margaret Jane Wyszomirski, eds. *America's Commitment to Culture, Government and the Arts*. Boulder: Westview Press, 1995.

Nabokov, Nicolas. *Bagázh: Memoirs of a Russian Cosmopolitan*. New York: Atheneum, 1975.

Ninkovich, Frank A. *The Diplomacy of Ideas: U.S. Foreign Policy and Cultural Relations, 1938-1950*. New York: Cambridge University Press, 1981.

————. *U.S. Information Policy and Cultural Diplomacy*. New York: Foreign Policy Association, 1996.

Noguchi, Isamu. *The Sculptor's World*. New York: Harper and Row, 1968.

Oshinsky, David M. *A Conspiracy So Immense: The World of Joe McCarthy*. New York: Free Press, 1983.

Payne, Charles. *American Ballet Theatre*. New York: Knopf, 1978.

Perrett, Geoffry. *A Dream of Greatness: The American People, 1945-1963*. New York: Coward, McCann and Geoghegan, 1979.

Pollack, Barbara, and Charles Humphrey Woodford. *Dance is a Moment: A Portrait of José Limón in Words and Pictures*. Pennington, N.J.: Princeton Book Company, 1993.

Public Papers of the Presidents, Dwight D. Eisenhower, 1954. Washington, D.C. Office of the Federal Register, National Archives Record Service, General Services Administration, 1960.

Pells, Richard. *Not Like Us: How Europeans Have Loved, Hated, and Transformed American Culture Since World War II*. New York: Basic Books, 1997.

Reeves, Richard. *President Kennedy: Profile of Power*. New York: Touchstone, 1993.

Reich, Cary. *The Life of Nelson A. Rockefeller: Worlds to Conquer 1908-1958*. New York: Doubleday, 1996.

Reynolds, Nancy. "The Red Curtain: Balanchine's Critical Reception in the Soviet Union." *Proceedings of the Society of Dance History Scholars*, 1992, pp. 47-57.

Richmond, Yale. *U.S.-Soviet Cultural Exchanges, 1958-1986*. Boulder: Westview Press, 1987.

Robinson, Harlow. *The Last Impresario*. New York: Viking, 1994.

Ross, Janice. "Innocence Abroad: The 1965 Stockholm Premiere of Anna Halprin's 'Parades and Changes.'" *Proceedings of the Society of Dance History Scholars*, 1992, pp. 159-168.

Rovere, Richard H. *Senator Joe McCarthy*. New York: Harcourt, Brace, 1959.

Schuster, Dr. J. Mark Davidson. *Supporting the Arts: An International Comparative Study*. Washington, D.C.: National Endowment for the Arts.

Samovar, Larry A., Richard E. Porter, and Nemi C. Jain. *Understanding Intercultural Communication*. Belmont, Calif: Wadsworth Publishing Company, 1981.

Siegel, Marcia B., ed. "Nik: A Documentary." *Dance Perspectives*, no. 48 (Winter 1971).

Signitzer, Benno H., and Timothy Coombs. "Public Relations and Public Diplomacy: Conceptual Convergence." *Public Relations Review*, 18, no. 2 (Summer 1992), pp. 137-147.

Solberg, Carl. *Riding High: America in the Cold War*. New York: Mason and Lipscomb, 1973.

Sorenson, Thomas C. *The Word War: The Story of American Propaganda*. New York: Harper and Row, 1968.

Sperber, A.M. *Murrow, His Life and Times*. New York: Freundlich Books, 1986.

Stearns, Marshall and Jean. *Jazz Dance: The Story of American Vernacular Dance*. New York: Macmillan, 1968.

Stewart, Edward, Samuel P. Huntington, Laura Nader, Mustafa Safwan, and Edward Said. *Can Cultures Communicate*. Washington, D.C.: American Enterprise Institute for Public Policy Research Round Table, 1976.

Straight, Michael. *Twigs for An Eagle's Nest: Government and the Arts, 1965-1978*. New York: Devon Press, 1979.

Stratyner, Barbara. *Ned Wayburn and the Dance Routine*. Studies in Dance History, no. 13 (1996).

Sugiyama, Yasushi, ed. *Between Understanding and Misunderstanding: Problems and Prospects for International Cultural Exchange*. New York: Greenwood Press, 1990.

Tallchief, Maria, with Larry Kaplan. *Maria Tallchief, America's Prima Ballerina*. New York: Holt, 1997.

Taper, Bernard. *Balanchine: A Biography*. 2nd rev. ed. Berkeley: University of California Press, 1996

Taylor, Paul. *Private Domain*. New York: Knopf, 1987.

Terry, Walter. *I Was There: Selected Dance Reviews and Articles 1936-1976*. New York: Dekker, 1978.

Thomson, Charles A., and Walter H.C. Laves. *Cultural Relations and U.S. Foreign Policy*. Bloomington: Indiana University Press, 1963.

Trumbo, Dalton. *Additional Dialogue 1942-1962*. New York: Evans, 1970.

Tuch, Hans. *Communicating with the World: U.S. Public Diplomacy Overseas*. New York: St. Martin's Press, 1990.

Valis Hill, Constance. "Katherine Dunham's *Southland*: Protest in the Face of Repression." *Dance Research Journal*, 26, no. 2 (Fall 1994), pp. 1-10.

Vaughan, David, "The Real Shock: The Merce Cunningham Dance Company's World Tour, 1964." *Proceedings of the Society of Dance History Scholars*, 1992, pp. 21-27.

———. "Merce Cunningham's *The Seasons*." *Dance Chronicle*, 18, no. 2 (1995), pp. 311–318

Von Eschen, Penny. *Race Against Empire: Black Americans and Anticolonialism 1937–1957*. Ithaca, N.Y.: Cornell University Press, 1997.

Vinacke, Harold M. *Far Eastern Politics in the Postwar Period*. New York: Appleton-Century-Crofts, 1956.

Walker, Martin. *The Cold War, A History*. New York: Holt, 1993.

Warner, Denis. *Reporting South-East Asia*. Sydney: Angus and Robertson, 1966.

Warren, Larry. *Anna Sokolow, The Rebellious Spirit*. Princeton: Princeton Book Company, 1991.

Whitfield, Stephen J. *The Culture of the Cold War*. Baltimore: Johns Hopkins University Press, 1991.

Wick, Charles Z. "The Future of Public Diplomacy." *Presidential Studies Quarterly*, 19, no. 1 (Winter 1989), pp. 25-30.

Wieck, Randolph. *Ignorance Abroad. American Educational and Cultural Foreign Policy and the Office of Assistant Secretary of State.* Westport, Conn.: Praeger, 1992.

Wyatt, Woodrow. *Southwards from China. A Survey of South East Asia Since 1945.* London: Hodder and Stoughton, 1952.

Videotapes

Below is a short list of commercially available videorecordings featuring works by some of the choreographers discussed in this book. The cassettes may be purchased from Princeton Book Company, P.O. Box 831, Hightstown, N.J. 08520-0831. Following each title is the release date; dates in parenthesis indicate the stage premiere and, if known, when the work was filmed or recorded.

ALVIN AILEY

An Evening with Alvin Ailey, 108 min., color, 1986. Includes Ailey's *Revelations* (1960) and Talley Beatty's *The Stack-Up* (1983).

GEORGE BALANCHINE

The Balanchine Library. Ten separate videos including the two-part *Balanchine Celebration*, filmed in 1993; *The Balanchine Essays* (arabesque, passé and attitude, port de bras and épaulement); Anne Bell's *Dancing for Mr. B: Six Balanchine Ballerinas* (1989); and four programs, originally aired on PBS, with excerpts of major Balanchine works such as *The Four Temperaments* (1946).

MERCE CUNNINGHAM

Cage/Cunningham, 95 min., color, 1991. Includes excerpts from Cunningham's *Summerspace* (1958), *Walkaround Time* (1968), and *RainForest* (1968).

Points in Space, 55 min., color, 1986. This work was one of Cunningham's late collaborations with Cage.

KATHERINE DUNHAM

Dance Black America, 87 min., color, 1990. Includes a revival of *Shango* (1945).

MARTHA GRAHAM

Martha Graham in Performance, 87 min., color, 1996. Includes *A Dancer's World* (1957), *Night Journey* (1947/1960), and *Appalachian Spring* (1944/1959), with Graham performing her original roles.

Three by Martha Graham, 93 min., b/w, 1988. Includes *Cortege of Eagles* (1967/1969), *Seraphic Dialogue* (1955/1969), and *Acrobats of God* (1960/1969).

ERICK HAWKINS

Erick Hawkins' America, 57 min., color with b/w sequences, 1992. Includes portions of his early work *Black Lake*, as well as excerpts from later works.

ALWIN NIKOLAIS

The World of Alwin Nikolais, 217 min., color, 1996. Five programs with more than thirty works from different periods, including the 1950s.

ANNA SOKOLOW
Anna Sokolow, Choreographer, 20 min., color and b/w, 1978. Includes an excerpt from *Rooms* (1955).

PAUL TAYLOR
Speaking in Tongues, 54 min., color, 1991. A revised version for television of the work that premiered in 1988.
The Wrecker's Ball, 56 min., color, 1996. Includes three recent works by Taylor— *Company B* (1991), *A Field of Grass* (1993), and *Funny Papers* (1994).

Three films that were used abroad by the USIA can be viewed on videotape at the film and video division of the National Archives. One is called *Limón in Singapore* and contains *The Moor's Pavane*. Another is *Limón's Legacy*, which was made by the USIA and contains excerpts from several works, all excellently shot. *Nik: Experience in Sight and Sound*, which was also made by the USIA, is an overview of Alwin Nikolais's work.

Index

Naima Prevots is a Professor of Dance at American University and the author of *American Pageantry: A Movement for Art and Democracy* (1990) and *Dancing in the Sun: Hollywood Choreographers, 1915–1937* (1987).

Library of Congress Cataloging-in-Publication Data

Prevots, Naima, 1935–
    Dance for export: cultural diplomacy and the Cold
    War / Naima Prevots ; introduction by Eric Foner.
        p.   cm. — (Studies in dance history)
    Includes bibliographical references (p.   ) and index.
    1. Dance—Political aspects—United States—History.
    2. Cultural relations. I. Title. II. Series: Studies in dance
    history.
    (Unnumbered)
    ISBN 0–8195–6365–X (cloth : alk. paper)
    ISBN 0–8195– 6464–8 (pbk : alk. paper)
    GV1623.P72   1998
    792.8'09—dc21   98–26434